PRAISE FOR *THRIVING IN THE EYE OF THE HURRICANE*

"You are about to embark on a hero's journey. You don't need to carry any special equipment with you to get started—in fact, you will find everything you need inside the pages of this book.

"Whether you've been called to this adventure by a direct or indirect experience of the pandemic, the global economic downturn, or the startling uncertainty of our times, by heeding the call, you are guaranteed a meeting with a mentor, and Joseph Bailey is the perfect mentor and guide for this particular journey."

—Michael Neill, author of *The Inside Out Revolution* and *The Space Within* (excerpted from the foreword)

" 'Is resilience truly natural?' 'Is it really so simple?' 'Do I actually have the capacity for peace and joy within me?'

"With clarity, skill and deep compassion, Joe Bailey answers these questions—'Yes'—and guides us gently toward one of the most important skills you will ever learn: *Thriving in the Eye of the Hurricane.*"

—Henry Emmons, MD, psychiatrist and author of *The Chemistry of Joy* and *The Chemistry of* Calm

"Joe Bailey's *Thriving in the Eye of the Hurricane* is a game changer that brings hope not only to psychology and psychiatry, but to the world and all who inhabit it."

—William F. Pettit, Jr., MD, retired psychiatrist and
Three Principles-based mental health educator,
adjunct clinical professor, Department of Psychiatry,
Creighton University School of Medicine

"Joe's book offers hope and inspiration to those who are suffering. He shows how transformation can happen for all of us from all walks of life when we are open to it. He shares with such simplicity and practicality, making the book so impactful."

—Danielle Guinaugh, MS, LMHC, NCC, MCAP, clinical director of
Gulf Breeze Recovery Center

"That there is an invisible, formless intelligence making life possible, running your mind, and ensuring a built-in resilience to any and all challenges is such good news. But is it hopeful speculation? Read this book and you will come away convinced that you are equipped to handle any 'hurricane.' It's not easy to describe and explain the invisible, yet Joe does it with clarity and simplicity. Absorb his words. Let the knowledge in this book sink in and you will discover the extraordinary, ordinary powers inside your own mind."

—Sandra Krot, human relations consultant at Insight Principles,
Inc., and coauthor of *Invisible Power: Insight Principles at Work*

"A thought-provoking great read that takes you on a journey of stories, examples that may at times seem a bit too simple, but we are continually pointed to the truth. In a world of such uncertainty, this is a brilliant companion of a book to help you roll with the changes and improve your experience in living your best life with much less effort. That calm in the storm that resides within us all is a fantastic navigation tool back to calmness."

—Louise O'Dalaigh, RN, healthcare leader and coach at the NHS (National Health Service), Northern Ireland. Learn more at louiseodalaigh.com

"If you want to not just feel better but handle challenges in life with more ease and wisdom, then look no further than this book! In these pages, Joe simply and clearly presents the missing link to resilience and navigating life's ups and downs. With Joe's words, this book opens up an already present but seldom embodied dimension to life, allowing you to stop surviving and start truly thriving."

—Rudi and Jules Kennard, international speakers and authors of *Wholality*. Learn more at www.innateevolution.com

THRIVING
IN THE
EYE
OF THE
HURRICANE

PREVIOUS BOOKS BY JOSEPH BAILEY

The Serenity Principle (HarperCollins, 1990)

Slowing Down to the Speed of Life,
with Dr. Richard Carlson (HarperCollins, 1996)

The Speed Trap (HarperCollins, 1999)

Slowing Down to the Speed of Love (McGraw-Hill, 2004)

*Fearproof Your Life: How to Thrive in a World
Addicted to Fear* (Conari Press, 2008)

Joseph's books have sold over a half million copies nationally and
are available internationally in twenty-six languages.

THRIVING
IN THE
EYE
OF THE
HURRICANE

UNLOCKING RESILIENCE IN TURBULENT TIMES

BY JOSEPH BAILEY, MA, LP

mango
PUBLISHING
CORAL GABLES

Cover Design: Roberto Nuñez
Layout & Design: Katia Mena
Interior Illustration: rfvectors.com / Adobe Stock

For permission requests, please contact the publisher at:
Mango Publishing Group
2850 S Douglas Road, 2nd Floor
Coral Gables, FL 33134 USA
info@mango.bz

For special orders, quantity sales, course adoptions and corporate sales,
please email the publisher at sales@mango.bz. For trade and wholesale
sales, please contact Ingram Publisher Services at customer.service@
ingramcontent.com or +1.800.509.4887.

Thriving in the Eye of the Hurricane: Unlocking Resilience in
Turbulent Times

Library of Congress Cataloging-in-Publication number: 2021942642
ISBN: (print) 978-1-64250-660-0, (ebook) 978-1-64250-661-7
BISAC category code SEL024000, SELF-HELP / Self-Management /
Stress Management

Printed in the United States of America

DEDICATION

I dedicate this book to my mentor of many decades, Sydney Banks.

This ordinary man had a profound transformational experience in 1973 that led to a paradigm shift in psychology and many other fields of study. Syd's talks, books, and recordings developed into what is now known as Three Principles Psychology. His students and mentees have taken their own transformations into many professions, helping thousands of people experience deep change in their lives. This book is one of hundreds written about this paradigm shift. I am grateful to Sydney, whose awakening triggered my own.

In deepest gratitude,
Joseph Bailey

TABLE OF CONTENTS

FOREWORD

BY MICHAEL NEILL

*"We shall not cease from exploration
And the end of all our exploring
Will be to arrive where we started
And know the place for the first time."*

—T.S. Eliot, *Four Quartets*

You are about to embark on a hero's journey. You don't need to carry any special equipment with you to get started—in fact, you will find everything you need inside the pages of this book.

Whether you've been called to this adventure by a direct or indirect experience of the pandemic, the global economic downturn, or the startling uncertainty of our times, by heeding the call, you are guaranteed a meeting with a mentor, and Joseph Bailey is the perfect mentor and guide for this particular journey.

I first came across Joe's work in another book he wrote many years ago with his friend Richard Carlson called *Slowing Down to the Speed of Life*. Although I came to that book with no prior understanding of the principles it shared, the title itself proved incredibly helpful to me. Since that time, I've had the privilege of spending time with, learning from, and even teaching alongside him, and my life has changed for the better in ways I didn't even know were possible.

As you read, you will cross the threshold of your ordinary world into the unknown. You will hear about many things you probably know something about, like "resilience" and "the power of thought," but if you allow yourself the space to get quiet while you read, those words will take on previously unimagined meanings.

For example, many of us think of resilience as a skill we can learn and master through mental toughness and daily practice. But in this book, Joe points to the fact that as children, we exhibited resilience before we could even pronounce the word. This suggests that our ability to bounce back from life's challenges is built into us from the moment we are born, and that it surfaces naturally in those moments when our "grown-up" thinking falls away.

Through a potpourri of insights, metaphors, and real-life examples, you will find that place inside of you that remains perfect, whole, calm, and clear even as your circumstances change and the dramas of life play out on a global stage.

And as you live more and more of the time from what I have come to call in my own life "the space within," your relationships begin to change for the better.

The first and most important of these is your relationship with yourself. You may notice yourself having more compassion for your foibles and more confidence that you don't need to know how you will handle something before it's time. You will come to see that you don't need to be driving the bus to enjoy the ride, and at times, it may be hard to tell whether life is getting easier or you're just getting better at living it.

Your recognition that each one of us is living in a separate thought-created reality will allow you to connect deeply with people's humanity, even when they think differently than you. Your relationship with others will naturally improve as you find yourself with less to prove.

And most hopefully of all, you will no longer be so afraid of the inevitable challenges and ordeals that we all must face from time to time. When we come to see that the obstacles in our path are simply stepping stones to a new way of being in the world, we welcome them as opportunities to raise our level of understanding and see the inside-out nature of experience at deeper and deeper levels.

As with any hero's journey, you will find many allies along the path; the dozens of real-life stories of people whose lives have been changed for the better by finding the "eye of the hurricane"—the calm in the center of the storm—are perhaps my favorite part of this book. And while some of these stories may seem "too good to be true" or even miraculous, that's more to do with the limits of our imagination than with any actual limitations on what's possible.

As Joe's mentor Syd Banks says in one of his stories about a woman working with gang members in Minnesota who overcame their differences and found ways to love and connect in the midst of some pretty terrible conditions, "Don't ever forget the miracles, dearie…"

My fondest hope for you is that you allow this book to guide you all the way along the journey through to its inevitable end—a return to your ordinary world having experienced an extraordinary shift in perception. Nothing may have changed, yet everything will seem different.

One of the many wonderful things about human beings is that when we see better, we do better. And the more of us who are doing better, the more we will all wake up to the beauty and possibility of the world.

With all my love,
Michael Neill, author of *The Inside-Out Revolution* and *The Space Within*

PART I

THE HURRICANE OF OUR NEW NORMAL: "WE ARE LIVING IN INTERESTING TIMES"

CHAPTER 1

LIVING IN THE HURRICANE

"In the middle of difficulty lies opportunity."

—John Archibald Wheeler, describing what he
termed Albert Einstein's "three rules of work"

As I write during these chaotic times, my heart goes out to people around the globe who are facing uncertainty and the fear of the unknown at present, as well as inevitable challenges in the future. Just yesterday, speaking to my editor on the phone, I could feel her angst as we discussed my book. I knew there were unprecedented wildfires burning in the Western United States, so I asked how she was doing.

"I'm a little freaked at the moment," she replied; "As I look out my window at the skyline of San Francisco, it's noon, but the sky is as black as the middle of the night. I need to find out what's happening." I could feel her fear. Millions of acres of forest, parks, towns, and cities were being engulfed by the worst wildfires in our history. Last night, the news was filled with one story after another of the destruction—record breaking wildfires in the Western states, growing numbers of dead from the Covid-19 pandemic, unfolding scandals and division in our presidential race, and the brand-new

Living Planet Report, which shows a massive reduction of animal communities on earth—84 percent just since 1970.

These are just a few of the challenges we face in the hurricane that is life as we are bombarded daily by terrifying news through various media. But we can learn to find the still point within ourselves: At the center of a hurricane with 200 mph destructive winds lies the "eye of the storm," a calm center where birds and planes can fly peacefully. In today's turbulence and negativity, how do we find the calm center of the hurricane?

> "The eye is a region of mostly calm weather at the center of tropical cyclones. The eye of a storm is a roughly circular area, typically 30–65 km (19–40 miles) in diameter. It is surrounded by the eye wall, a ring of towering thunderstorms where the most severe weather and highest winds occur. The cyclone's lowest barometric pressure occurs in the eye and can be as much as 15 percent lower than the pressure outside the storm."
>
> —Wikipedia

Our minds are like hurricanes, often whirling around with growing insecurity and turmoil as we worry about how to make a living, raise our children, and adapt to the changes of our uncertain times. The wonderful thing is that we also have a still calm center at the heart of our being, which is the source of our resilient mind. This part of us is a compass of wisdom that can guide us in moving through the unknown future and the challenges of our daily lives. Pilots will tell you that flying through the eye wall into the eye of the hurricane can be a rocky ride, but once within the center, they experience breathtaking peacefulness and beauty. So it is with us as we discover the "eye" of our mind, that core of being which is full of love, peace, and understanding. We can learn to thrive in spite of the high winds, guided by the insight and wisdom of this calm center.

No matter how furious the winds of our individual thoughts may be, the center of our being remains, waiting for us to listen and discover peace of mind, sanity, and hope. We can call this "eye" resilience, mental health, our True Self, or our divine guidance. Many of us have no idea that this inner resource resides within us. For much of my life, I didn't know it either. But once I understood how my own unique experience of life is being created by psychological processes, I began to experience my resilience more and more. I was fortunate to be exposed to a new psychological paradigm which points to the underlying principles of human experience. This allowed me to find the eye of the hurricane within my own being.

For the past forty years, I have been teaching and writing about these Principles in my practice as a clinical psychologist and addictions therapist, writer, teacher, and consultant to organizations. My goal has been to pass on the discoveries that allow me consistent access to my resilient nature, especially during these uncertain times. I have learned how to live with less stress while thriving in the eye of the hurricane. I have taught these Principles to people from around the world—people from all walks of life suffering from addictions and mental health issues, including corporate leaders, medical professionals, counselors, and social service workers. I want to share this secret both through my own story and through stories from thousands of others whose lives have been transformed by this understanding.

The purpose of this book is for readers to gain an understanding of how their minds work and to come to know that all the answers they seek lie within the "eye" of their own minds. My hope is that each of us will experience being guided by our innate resilience through our own hurricanes into that safe place of peace and insight.

A BRIEF HISTORY OF HUMAN TRANSFORMATION AND SOCIETAL SHIFTS: LIFE INTERRUPTED LEADS TO OPENNESS AND NEW THINKING

Throughout time, human beings have gone through periods of great challenge, adversity, and turmoil similar to what we are facing in our current era. These periods force us to reconsider our lives—to reflect, listen to our inner voice of wisdom and insight, and create a new reality.

For example, prior to the Renaissance, Europe was devastated by the Black Death (bubonic plague) circa 1350 AD, which wiped out huge swaths of the population of Italy, France, England, and other European countries. It was also a time of extreme corruption in the Catholic Church, epitomized by the reign of Pope Alexander VI in the late fifteenth century (1492–1503), who kept a mistress in the Vatican, along with their four children, was involved with illegal political activity, and amassed a fortune in land and riches.

This led to a new age we know as the Renaissance. The fourteenth and fifteenth centuries produced some of the greatest artists, scientists, and inventors ever, such as Leonardo DaVinci and Michelangelo. Greek and Roman classics were brought back, and schools and universities sprang up all over what was becoming the modern European world. Free thinking and creativity were encouraged, which widely influenced political transformations in both western and eastern Europe, and eventually led to the birth of modern democracy and the breakdown of the powerful monarchies of Europe. This was also the time of the Reformation, beginning with Martin Luther's 95 Theses in 1517 questioning the authority and the infallibility of the Catholic Church, which formed the basis of Protestantism.

Disease periodically erupted into massive epidemics and plagues in the sixteenth and seventeenth centuries as great discoveries continued to emerge. It was during this time that the ideas of Rene Descartes (1596–1650) gave rise to the Age of Enlightenment. His famous saying, "Cogito ergo sum"—"I think, therefore I am"—was instrumental in creating the Age of Reason. And Sir Francis Bacon (1561–1626) is credited with the development of the scientific method, leading to the Scientific Revolution. Mathematical and philosophical advancements advanced the Age of Enlightenment when Sir Isaac Newton published his *Principia Mathematica* in 1687 and John Locke's *Essay Concerning Human Understanding* saw print in 1689.

The Great Plague (1665–1666) was the worst outbreak of bubonic plague in England since the Black Death epidemic of 1348. London lost roughly 15 percent of its population. Young Isaac Newton, then an average student at Cambridge's Trinity College, was forced to return to his childhood home. What looked like an unfortunate circumstance led to one of the greatest scientific developments in the modern era.

In the quiet of his home surroundings and away from educational constraints, Isaac Newton's creativity flourished. He filled notebooks with revolutionary ideas and calculations. The time of "The Great Plague" was thought to be a medical and societal disaster, but for Newton, it was a time of retreat that he used to bring forth new ideas.

Newton created a future for science that changed humanity's view of the world, ushering in a paradigm shift toward Newtonian physics. He created differential and integral calculus, formulated a theory of universal gravitation, explored optics, and conducted experiments with prisms investigating light. Sir Isaac Newton's innate resilience led us into the Industrial Revolution's advancements in science and technology, including laborsaving machines, airplanes, space travel, and more.

I believe we are now in a time that is fertile for another major leap in our evolution as human beings. Given the catastrophic challenges we now face, we need another shift in consciousness for the sake of all humanity. All of our success in building economic prosperity has led to overpopulation, the climate crisis, polarization within our societies, economic disparity, the threat of a global nuclear war, and the many medical crises arising from the current pandemic, HIV, the opioid and alcoholism epidemics, and on and on. The world is in a mess, and it has painted us into a corner where the only way out is *up*.

What do I mean by "the only way out is up"? What I am saying is that the present turmoil is our own fault. Rather than using our minds in a wise and insightful way, we have tended to be blinded by the short-sighted and selfish ego and have lost sight of the bigger picture. To quote a popular paraphrase of Albert Einstein's philosophy: We cannot solve our problems with the same thinking we used when we created them.

The only way out of our current age of anxiety and turmoil is through a deeper understanding of the principles behind our everyday psychological functioning. If we humans don't shift the level of our consciousness through a deeper understanding of how our mind works, we will continue down the same self-destructive path.

As the old saying goes, "The definition of madness is doing the same thing over and over and expecting a different result." We need new thinking borne of insight and wisdom to make more intelligent societal decisions for ourselves and our wider community. The only way this is possible is through a deeper understanding of the fundamental principles of human psychology. Although our past successes have led to the most affluent, prosperous societies in history, huge numbers still suffer from poverty and all of its debilitating consequences. In spite of many successes, all of us face extinction through climate change, nuclear war, and the destruction of our planet's ecosystems. We must once again reflect and listen to the wisdom that lies within each of us. We must each learn to live from our resilient self—the source of insight that leads us to a better, safer, and more loving future.

MY STORY OF LIVING IN THE EYE OF THE HURRICANE

Allow me to tell my personal story and how I came to understand the principles that help me to thrive in the eye of the hurricane.

I grew up in a rural Midwestern community and was fortunate to have been well-provided for by loving parents within a large family and to have had access to good schools. Although my family was successful in many ways, communication between family members was unhealthy. For instance, my dad and his brother had irreconcilable differences; this created unspoken tension that affected both the family and the family-run nursery business.

Finally, after a long court battle, my dad bought his brother out. I felt the tension but didn't know its source, and as a result, I was anxious and fearful as a child.

Later in my teens, my anxiety led me to develop great curiosity about psychology and spiritual studies. I read many books on the subject and was greatly influenced by the missionary work of my Aunt Milly, a Maryknoll nun in Guatemala and Mexico, and of my Uncle Bud, a Maryknoll priest in Bolivia. They helped the indigenous people not only spiritually, but they lent them much needed practical support, such as providing clean water and sourcing income-generation possibilities.

My aunt arranged for me to be an exchange student in high school while she was in living in Guatemala as the mother superior of her order in Central America. I lived with my Guatemalan exchange family and spent time with my aunt, plus other nuns and priests whom I very much admired. I fell in love with the idea of service and dreamed of compassionately working together with those less fortunate than me. This formative experience inspired me to consider becoming a priest or a Christian brother, following in the footsteps of my aunt and uncle.

After high school, I chose to spend a year in seminary to prepare for the priesthood; but after a few months, I realized that life as a priest was not my calling. In my sophomore year of college, I began undergraduate studies in psychology and later went on to graduate studies. I became licensed as a clinical psychologist and began my career as a therapist and trainer in the addictions field. By the end of my twenties, I was traveling the country, teaching counselors in the family therapy and addictions fields through the renowned Johnson Institute in Minnesota. I later started a private

practice in Minneapolis specializing in aftercare for families with
addiction issues.

However, my own mental health suffered while I was helping others
to regain theirs. I was stressed, and my own marriage failed when I
was age twenty-eight, even after a great deal of traditional couple's
therapy. No matter how many books I read or how many seminars
and workshops I attended, happiness, contentment, and inner peace
eluded me. I practiced yoga and meditation and went on retreats,
but nothing seemed to last in terms of my well-being. By age
twenty-nine, I was burned out and disillusioned with my profession.
I felt like one of "the blind leading the blind." I entered into personal
therapy and joined support groups, but the only answer that I got
to my pain was that I was a victim of my past, which I had to work
through, perhaps for the rest of my life.

THE TURNING POINT

Then in 1980, at age thirty-three, my life changed course
completely. At the invitation of a friend from graduate school,
Dr. Keith Blevens, I attended a seminar by Sydney Banks at the
University of Miami Medical School. Sydney, who was a welder
by trade with only a ninth grade education, had experienced an
epiphany in 1973 that totally changed his life. Some psychologists
looking for mental health breakthroughs through a National
Institute of Mental Health grant had discovered Mr. Banks and
heard of the incredible transformations that were happening for
troubled people who listened to him speak. My friend Dr. Keith
Blevens was one of those psychologists.

Before I met Syd, I was anxious, depressed, unable to keep a
relationship going, and frantically searching for answers to the

question of life's meaning. I had grown cynical and was pessimistic that I would ever find an answer, often fantasizing at the time about leaving my profession. I was reluctant to meet Syd Banks, but for some reason, when my friend invited me to hear him speak, I felt strangely drawn to hear him. Something moved me in spite of my cynicism and hopelessness.

I had never met a man like Sydney Banks, and I had met some of the best psychologists and therapists in the country as well as religious and spiritual leaders. His message was simple and profound, and it impacted me very deeply. Yet it scared me, because it shook the foundations of my well-honed beliefs about psychology and why happiness was impossible. I was a seminar leader and trainer at a very young age for my profession, and I'd studied with the best, yet Syd's simple wisdom and his certainty pulled the rug out from under everything I had come to believe. Listening to him that first night at an informal dinner provoked a dual reaction within me. Part of me heard truth in his words, and my whole being calmed down at this recognition, but at the same time my ego/intellect felt challenged and threatened and I wanted to escape and run out of the room.

With each challenging question that came to my mind, he would intuitively sense and answer it in his next sentence. It felt like he was reading my mind. It spooked me out, and I wanted to flee. But at the same time, I felt riveted to his words, sensing I had found the missing piece to a puzzle I had been searching for all my life.

My mind whirled around, pitting Syd's simple Truth against my fortress of hollow intellectual concepts and ideas. Suddenly I felt a return to the happiness of early childhood, a feeling of lighthearted joy. I found the peace that I had been looking for, deep inside my own self.

This period of time was the birth of a new paradigm in psychology, though few realized it. In the past four decades, I have seen this understanding grow from merely influencing a handful of professionals into a worldwide phenomenon, one that is not only changing psychology but impacting educational systems, healthcare, correctional institutions, community revitalization, psychotherapy, coaching, business culture and organizational consulting, religious organizations, and the general public. You will be able to learn more about these changes across a variety of fields in Part IV of this book. At a Three Principles international conference in London last year, there were attendees from thirty-eight countries.

I have written five books on Three Principles Psychology that have sold over a half million copies. There are hundreds of other books, videos, webinars, websites, films, and other educational media available based on this paradigm. My book *Slowing Down to the Speed of Life*, with Dr. Richard Carlson, is in print in twenty-six languages. Dr. Carlson authored *Don't Sweat the Small Stuff*, which has sold over 20 million copies. I have had the privilege to speak all over the world on this new understanding. Thousands of people have had transformational experiences as a result of discovering and realizing these fundamental principles. They are thriving and living with more resilience.

Sydney's teachings have cured my burnout, and because of the Principles, my career has gone down a totally new path, allowing me to widely share this new understanding of the human experience. For this I am extremely grateful. I have worked with addiction treatment centers, and I have taught Three Principles Psychology in many universities; I have also worked with many large healthcare institutions counseling doctors and nurses, who suffer from an epidemic level of burnout. I have also provided consulting to social service agencies, police, firefighters, teachers, and business organizations and am part of a wave of new professionals who are helping people alleviate unnecessary suffering caused by a misunderstanding of the mind.

It seems to me that this paradigm discovery will have a greater impact than the major discoveries of the physical sciences that led to the industrial, technological, and digital revolutions. The reason for this is because most of the problems we face in this world are unintentionally mind-made, due in large part to a huge innocent misunderstanding of human psychological functioning.

My discoveries that weekend with Sydney Banks gave me the psychological Principles to begin my own transformational experience. For me, the shift was gradual yet profound; my life has blossomed with ongoing positive results—finding true love in a marriage of thirty-nine years, discovering a renewal of my career vocation, experiencing miracles in my work, and being overwhelmed by the response to my books from my readers. Little by little, insight by insight, I have gradually realized Syd's Principles for myself.

HOW THE THREE PRINCIPLES HAVE WORKED IN MY LIFE

First, I needed to realize that I wasn't broken, damaged, or flawed. My True Self is resilient, powerful, wise, and loving. Second, the Principles taught me how my psychological experience is totally connected to my thinking and emotions, which in turn create all my perceptions of the present, the past, and the future. In effect, I began to see that my entire life is connected to thought. Third, I realized that my psychological experience of life comes from my internal thinking, not what I am thinking about. Seeing this fundamental truth allowed me to no longer feel like a victim of my past, my genetics, or the circumstances of my surroundings.

With these realizations, I could see that the unknown future no longer had the power to make me anxious and afraid. I saw that my life was no longer determined by my past history. It became clear to me that even my thoughts and beliefs did not have power over me. I was free of the past and the future, bringing me into the present moment. I could learn from my past but not be held captive by it. I could imagine, dream, and prepare for the future through insight. I could recognize that worry and fear about any future possible scenarios were only thoughts, not the truth. Consequently, I could relax into the understanding that human beings are designed for moment-to-moment insight, and that this insight will assist them in any and all situations.

This isn't to say that my transformation happened in an instant. It is still happening even as I write this book. My insights happen in the moment, but for me, transformation is ongoing and a gradual process of self-realization, one insight at a time.

I will explore Three Principles Psychology to a much greater extent in Part II of this book so that you will gain the understanding that I did. In Part III, I will go deeper into the Principles behind transformational experiences and the process of personal evolution that leads to positive change not only in our own lives, but in those whose lives we touch and influence.

What Syd Banks discovered would end the duality between the psychological and spiritual worlds. He realized through his epiphany that there are three fundamental Principles of human existence—the very essence of our psychological experience of life. He realized that we are all part of the universal intelligence of all things—*Mind*. I will talk about how *Mind*, as a Principle, comes into relationship with us in our lives creating our psychological experience. (Throughout the book, when I am referring to the Three Principles, I will capitalize the word Principles.)

Mind is the catalyst that brings the power of *Thought* and *Consciousness* into existence as our human reality. Without these three powers or Principles, we could not experience the world of form—the physical world in which we live. Through this realization, Syd Banks erased the duality of Mind and Spirit and saw them as one and the same.

The word psychology comes from the Greek word 'psyche,' which means mind, soul, and spirit. Thus psychology is the study of mind, soul, and spirit. Traditional psychology has ignored Mind, the spiritual power behind all perceptions, all emotions, and all behavior. In actuality, these Principles are the missing link in our understanding of the human psychological experience.

The Principles are the compass that guides us back home to the innate resilience that is the essence of who we all are, no exceptions. Throughout this book, I will show you how to use this compass to guide you through the unknowns of your unique circumstances in our collective age of turmoil and uncertainty—be they illness, addiction, poverty, hardship, or a sense of emptiness in the midst of material abundance.

Although you will each walk your journey alone, the Principles of human experience will be your guide and map. Imagine yourself as an explorer going into the wilderness; you may get lost but will find your way again and again with the knowledge of navigation. You are never lost, even though moving through the uncharted unknown. Let us continue this journey together.

PART II

THE SOLUTION: REAWAKENING OUR INNATE RESILIENCE

CHAPTER 2

RESILIENCE: THE KEY TO THRIVING IN THE EYE OF THE HURRICANE

"The ultimate measure of a man is not where he stands in moments of comfort and convenience, but where he stands at times of challenge and controversy."

—Dr. Martin Luther King Jr.

Alexander Hamilton was born into challenging circumstances. He was born out of wedlock in Charlestown, West Indies; orphaned as a child, young Alexander was taken in by a prosperous merchant. When he was in his youth, a hurricane hit the island, and he wrote an apocalyptic fire-and-brimstone sermon for the town newspaper. He claimed that the divine purpose of the hurricane was to punish humans for their vanity and pomposity. The essay so impressed community leaders that they took up a collection and sent young Alexander to the North American colonies for further education. The rest is history. He played a prominent role in the creation of the United States Constitution and was a leader in the revolutionary war against the British king. Out of the hurricane's destruction arose an inspiration that would transform the world. His sharp intellect and persuasive writings helped to form the new United States of America.

Against all odds, young Alexander's potential as a statesman, coauthor of the constitution, and military mastermind was unleashed when that storm hit the West Indies. His resilience helped him break through the hurricane's wall into the calm eye of the storm. His passionate, prolific speaking and writing formed the basis of the famous Broadway musical *Hamilton*.

How is it that adversity is quite often the impetus for transformation and the awakening of our innate resilience? For most of us, our innate True Self is covered from view until we are challenged by a life crisis. In order to cope, we must rise to the occasion and in so doing, we discover our inner strength. How is it that our birthright of resilience remains hidden until something or someone "wakes us up"?

TRUTH AND THE THREE GODS

According to an old Hindu legend, There was once a time when all human beings were gods, but they so abused their divinity that Brahma, the chief god, decided to take it away from them and hide it where it could never be found.

Where to hide their divinity, that was the question. So Brahma called a council of the gods to help him decide. "Let's bury it deep in the earth," said the other gods. But Brahma answered, "No, that will not do, because humans will dig into the earth and find it." Then the gods said, "Let's sink it in the deepest ocean." But Brahma said, "No, not there, for they will learn to dive into the ocean and will find it." Then the gods said, "Let's take it to the top of the highest mountain and hide it there." But once again Brahma replied, "No, that will not do either, because they will eventually climb every mountain and once again take up their divinity." Then the gods gave up, saying, "We do not know where to hide it, because it seems that there is no place on earth or in the sea that human beings will not eventually reach."

Brahma thought for a long time; then he said, "Here is what we will do. We will hide their divinity deep in the center of their own being, for humans will never think to look for it there."

All the gods agreed that this was the perfect hiding place, and the deed was done. And since that time humans have been going up and down the earth, digging, diving, climbing, and exploring—searching for something already within themselves.

Human beings have searched for truth, peace of mind, fulfillment, and meaning outside themselves since the beginning of time. What if the Brahma was right and that which we have been searching for is within us?

The premise of this book is that we are all born with innate mental health, or what we refer to as *resilience*. There are no exceptions. We are all capable of experiencing peace of mind, wisdom, and a sense of connection to something greater than our personal ego.

It is part of our human experience to forget this, and we get lost in searching outside of ourselves to change how we feel. It is human to doubt ourselves, to ignore our own wisdom, and to misunderstand how to access the inner guidance system that is given to us all as our birthright.

Just observe young children, who quickly get over their upsets and bounce back to contentment and joy. They are living from their innate resilience. We have innocently learned to cover up our innate capacity for peace of mind and resilience with our thoughts, habits, beliefs, and prejudices (commonly known as the ego). Once we lose our connection to our true selves, we begin an infinite search outside ourselves for that natural feeling of well-being. We strive for success, power, control, and financial security while numbing ourselves with mind-altering substances. It seems that we will do anything that will give us even a momentary facsimile of a positive feeling.

The following is a story which illustrates how the power of resilience is always available, in this case during a tragic event in Nepal—one of the worse earthquakes in its history.

MAHIMA'S STORY

Mahima is a crisis response trainer from Nepal whose job is to prepare organizations for disasters and emergencies. A year before a devastating earthquake hit her country, she worked to understand the psychological side of disasters by searching the Internet for solutions. She was particularly interested in how people keep their bearings during the dangerous situations in front of them. She saw that no matter how well crisis responders knew their protocols, when they were stressed or burned out, mistakes were made and lives were lost.

Mahima's Internet search led her to discover a series of talks on Three Principles Psychology, which posits among other things that psychological stress is linked not to circumstances and events outside the person, but to the individual's thinking in the moment. One line she heard in the seminar stayed with her: "We are always living in the feeling of our thinking in the moment."

When Nepal was struck by the earthquake a year later, Mahima discovered an important lesson about resilience. She found that whether she reacted with tension or calmness to the crisis directly correlated to her moment-by-moment state of mind.

The following is a paraphrase of her story:

> "There was destruction and devastation all around us after the first earthquake struck—nine thousand people were killed, and thousands more were injured or left homeless. We were overwhelmed with grief and fear as we watched this beautiful country pounded into a pile of rubble.
>
> "My family and I were huddled together in my home. With each tremor we were filled with terror, anticipating the next earthquake. Between tremors, we would wait in fear and imagine what might happen next. In contrast, my three-year-old niece would go back to playing between tremors and seemed to enjoy having her whole family together in one place. Her laughter and play relieved and distracted us momentarily from our own panicky feelings.
>
> "At one point, she looked at all of us and proclaimed, 'It's over, don't you see, it's over!' Her childlike innocence and lightheartedness in the face of our stress hit me like another earthquake—a psychological one. She was being resilient in the face of danger while the rest of us were feeling traumatized.
>
> "The dormant thought that had been resting in my head for many months suddenly burst forth—'We are always living in the feeling of our thinking each moment.' By witnessing my niece's resilience in the face of real

danger, I realized what the Three Principles Psychology was all about. With this insight, my mind and my body became calm.

"From that moment on, my stress diminished and my resilience returned. I realized that the earthquake and tremors didn't create my stress and fears, my thinking did. Since that profound moment, I have felt more energy and more clarity of thinking, and I am better able to respond to real and present dangers.

"Everybody did what they could to bring solace and help restore resilience in their communities in the weeks following the earthquake. I hosted webinars with international experts in the crisis response field and invited trainers from the UK to introduce these Principles in Nepal to help earthquake survivors source their own resilience more effectively. Many organizations, groups, and institutions such as schools, chambers of commerce, insurance companies, community hospitals, young women's leadership programs, and more have since benefitted from this teaching."

This same simple insight has been passed on to hundreds of people and is making a huge difference in the aftermath of this devastation. Since then, Mahima has worked toward bringing this understanding to many people and organizations in crisis. That has had a huge impact on people's ability to empathize, engage, and excel in the face of extreme difficulties.

As one aid worker stated, "I used to only be able to spend about two weeks in the field helping communities deal with the devastation and then I couldn't take it any longer. After I realized that my thinking baggage wasn't coming from the circumstances but from my thoughts in the moment, I was much more present in my service to others—I had more energy and was able to sleep more soundly. I can now spend six weeks in the field and come back energized and inspired instead of burned out."

THE NATURE OF RESILIENCE

Resilience is the capacity of human beings to respond in the moment to any challenge they face with insightful, innovative, and creative thinking, and to rebound more quickly when they lose their bearings. It is also the ability to envision new possibilities and solutions regardless of circumstances. In times of turmoil and challenges, we are prompted to tap into our innate resilience and learn to survive, and yes, even to thrive.

When we respond with stress, fear, and a sense of being overwhelmed, our thinking often becomes muddled and we can't see the situation with clarity. When we are able to keep our emotional balance in the face of adversity, we are better able to effortlessly rise to the occasion with courage and grace.

For example, many of my clients and colleagues have exhibited resilient responses during these past several months of the pandemic. Although challenges in dealing with work, children's education, and personal finances have been unnerving and stressful, most who have an understanding of these Principles are getting back on their feet more quickly and actually seeing this as a great opportunity to reflect and recreate themselves. They feel gratitude for the chance to attain a higher perspective and come out better than before.

RESILIENCE IS POWERFUL, SIMPLE, AND NATURAL

In today's world of uncertainty—challenged by pandemics, economic uncertainty, climate change and disasters, divisive politics, and the breakdown of our institutions—we can't predict the future with any confidence or control the demands on our time and energy. Our internal resilience is the key to not only dealing with the increased pressure, but also to thinking insightfully and resourcefully in response to any challenge. A clear head and a calm mind make us more intelligent, creative, and productive. We think smarter, not harder.

Mahima's story illustrates the power of resilience in dangerous circumstances. Resilience is always available in all circumstances, no matter how ordinary. It exposes and pushes aside the seemingly innocuous but constant drips of bother and insecurity that wear on our minds and health without being noticed. Resilience allows us to overcome challenges with more poise, clarity, energy, and compassion. We rise above our burned-out and over-stressed selves.

The best-kept secret for facing all the pressures of our modern society is that we have a built-in default setting of resilience already within us. We may have never learned to recognize this innate power because we misunderstand the source of our psychological experience of life.

The way the mind works is through the power of thought: We each perceive our life circumstances based on our unique thinking in the moment. We all have different thoughts based on our past experiences, beliefs, prejudices, and insightful lessons from our personal history. Each of us is dealt a different hand in our individual life experiences. However, we also have an ability to see our own thoughts from an insightful perspective, that is, we can realize *that* we are thinking. We may perceive certain thoughts to be beyond our control and dismiss them as off base, untrue, silly, unnecessary, or self-destructive. Once we are conscious that we are having a thought, what we choose to do with this thought is the most salient factor in our psychological experience and our ability to thrive.

DON'T BELIEVE EVERYTHING YOU THINK

I have a T-shirt that says, "Don't Believe Everything You Think!" I often use this slogan at my seminars and coaching sessions. A momentary pause before we act on our thoughts makes room for wisdom to enter. This short break in our thinking stream can help us discern where various thoughts are originating. Are they coming from my insecurity or from calm resolve, from wisdom or my habitual thought system? When we have a moment of clarity inside our own personal thinking, we are able to let an insecure thought pass and avoid needless suffering.

Mahima was finally able to realize that her fearful thoughts were not "caused" by the tremors of the earthquake but stemmed from her own worries about what would happen next. When she saw that her experience of fear was the result of her own internal thinking, not the earthquake, she immediately calmed down and was able to act decisively. This shows the power of resilience.

MISUNDERSTANDING THE NATURE OF THE HUMAN EXPERIENCE IS THE CAUSE OF OUR PSYCHOLOGICAL DISTRESS

Resilience is an innate capacity we all possess. Unfortunately, it has often been stifled by misunderstanding what actually causes our inner experience. Most approaches to stress prevention focus on developing certain coping mechanisms and qualities to become more resilient. Many times, these coping mechanisms fade over time or turn into another source of stress. They become burdensome to-do list items added to our already full plates.

This book focuses us in a totally different direction, that of understanding the underlying invisible Principles that govern how we experience our resilience in the moment. Rather than teaching techniques to cope with stress, this book will show you how to actually thrive during difficult times. You can learn to prevent stress from occurring or spiraling out of control by recognizing its root cause.

RESILIENCE IS A TOTALLY NATURAL STATE IN HUMAN BEINGS

We have erroneously reserved resilience as a trait of special gifted people, one rarely available to the average person. However, when observing young children, it is clear that they have a natural resilience. They get over things more quickly than adults, their emotions come and go, they are open to others, they bounce back from adversity more quickly, and they have a natural quality of curiosity that spurs them to learn from their mistakes.

As we go through life, we innocently learn to misuse the powers of Mind and Thought. We ruminate about past events, worry about the future, and become self-conscious and insecure. We tend to block our natural state of resilience by misunderstanding where feelings come from.

Many of us love to be around young children because they emanate resilience, joy, unconditional love, living in the moment, endless curiosity, and spontaneous happiness.

Dr. Amy Johnson, a Three Principles psychologist and author, was recently talking with me about this.

> "I remember as a child thinking, why are adults so serious? Why don't they just have fun? Then when I became an adult and adopted the same serious and anxious thinking, I developed an anxiety and eating disorder. After trying many types of therapy, I still was experiencing yet another panic attack or binge eating episode. I sought out a Three Principles counselor, and remarkably, my eating disorder and panic attacks vanished. Now, when I lapse into a slight case of worry, my resilient five-year-old gently reminds me, 'Mommy, why are you being so serious?' These words stop me in my tracks, and I realize that her wisdom is already intact. This is resilience in its natural state."

The late Dr. Richard Carlson, the author of *Don't Sweat the Small Stuff* and a dear friend of mine, told me the story of his wise and resilient six-year-old daughter Jazzy. One day he was grousing to his wife Kris about an upcoming dinner they had planned with friends who often argued politics. Jazzy interrupted and innocently asked, "Daddy, why don't you wait to have a bad time till you get there?"

WE HAVE ALL WITNESSED RESILIENCE

We have often seen someone who rises to the occasion and faces a crisis with extreme courage, intelligence, and clear thinking when others around them are panicking. We have also had moments when we surprised ourselves with how well we handled a difficult situation, responding with an unexplainable instinct or an approach that is out of the ordinary. As you learn more about the Principles of resilience, looking back, you will recognize many more of these magical moments in your life and in the lives of others.

Before I rediscovered my natural resilience, I occasionally experienced moments as a psychotherapist where I was "in the zone." My client would experience transformative impact as I spoke from a deep place within that had nothing to do with my training or experience. These moments felt elusive and mysterious at the time, but now I see that my natural resilient intelligence was responding in the moment to my client's needs. These times of deeper connection appeared to me then to be a fluke; now I know that they were not.

We occasionally hear news stories of heroic people saving others without concern for their own well-being. They are portrayed as "exceptional," but when they are interviewed, they are often humble, explaining that they don't know where their internal strength or courage came from. They see themselves as ordinary, doing what anyone would do in the same situation. Actually, this is true; this latent resilience lies within each of us.

When the attack occurred on 9/11 and terrorists hit the Twin Towers of New York, panic ensued as people frantically tried to escape the collapsing buildings. On one of the top floors, several executives crammed into an elevator along with a window washer named Juan Cordero to flee for safety. When the elevator suddenly stopped between floors, everybody panicked except Juan, who stayed calm and clearheaded. He pried the doors open and began to strike the sheetrock wall in front of them; then the others took turns until they had torn open a hole large enough to escape. By some miracle, they found a stairway and fled to safety. Juan's leadership and resilience in the face of extreme danger saved their lives. If not for his calm insight, the elevator would have been their tomb.

RESILIENCE IS NOT AN ACTION WE TAKE OR AN ACCOMPLISHMENT

Resilience is like a beach ball. We can hold it down under the water, but as soon as we release our grip, it immediately rises to the surface. We don't have to lift the beach ball; it rises according to the principles of physics. Resilience is not something we "do," but something that automatically rises when we remove the thinking that is holding it down.

At a conference I was hosting this past weekend on addictions and the Principles of resilience, one of the panelists shared a powerful story.

Derrik had been in prison for drugs and gang related violence. While in prison, he went through an addiction program called Beyond Recovery. He became an addiction coach, and after release from prison, started a program for families of inmates called Beyond Truth.

One day, he and his business partner were on the road driving somewhere when they came upon a crowd of people who were obviously upset. They saw a man lying in a pool of blood with a knife sticking out of him.

One man was crazy with rage, screaming, "I'm gonna kill whoever did this!" Derrik felt anger rising within himself too, but realized he needed to remain calm. A rush of compassion flooded over him, and without hesitation, he ran over to the man and hugged him. The man stopped screaming and started to weep in Derrik's arms. Derrik was taken aback by the sudden change as they were each touched by compassion in a volatile situation. Love had come to the surface. They were witnessing resilience in the face of violence.

OUR NATURAL PSYCHOLOGICAL IMMUNE SYSTEM

In my seminars on resilience, participants are usually looking for a technique or a formula to follow so that they can summon it at will. But resilience is more of an innate capacity—an inborn ability to right ourselves when we lose our balance. It is like the invisible immune system of the body, one that without our awareness or conscious control, rushes to the rescue to ward off an invading infection. Our immune system is a naturally occurring process, but it can be compromised when we misuse our bodies, become overly stressed, or don't take proper care of our health.

Resiliency is our psychological immune system. It allows us to put life into proper perspective, to let go of unnecessary thinking, to forgive and forget, and to not take life or the opinions of others too personally or seriously. We are able to focus in the moment, connect to others, and come to insights as needed for learning, responding, and living our lives. We already know how to be resilient, we have simply suppressed this instinctual knowledge with habitual insecure thinking.

When our resilience does show up in the moment, we can't really take credit. We feel fortunate, inspired, surprised, grateful, and humbled. Like clouds that float away to reveal the sunshine, unnecessary thinking begins to fall away, and we are returned to our natural state. Our resilience is like the sun: always present, just momentarily hidden.

Molly is a family practice physician in a large healthcare system. After three years in her role, she felt overwhelmed with balancing the increasing demands of her job and the equally demanding roles of being a wife and a mother to her three children. When she saw that her organization was offering a course on resiliency to address burnout, she jumped at the chance.

> "It was eye-opening to realize the power that my thoughts have over my day-to-day feelings. In particular, I realized how physically and emotionally draining it is when my mind is going a thousand miles an hour. Recognizing my ever-present resilience was a gradual process. I now catch myself going down the path of stressful thinking and remind myself that there is nothing productive in it.

> "Before the resilience seminar, it looked like so much was constantly coming at me from so many different directions. Now I think I have a better grasp of where my experience is coming from: the inside of my own thinking in the moment. I know that if I do what I'm doing now and stay present, things are going to be okay. I feel more in control. I don't feel like all the stuff coming at me is beyond me anymore."

After the seminar, Molly went from getting only three to four hours of sleep per night to six to eight hours a night. She was able to cut down her workday by several hours due to her mind being clearer, which in turn led to better time management and healthier boundaries. Her calm in the eye of the hurricane allowed her to renew her vocational enthusiasm and achieve a better work/ life balance.

In this new normal of chaos and uncertainty in a world of never-ending changes, we need the compass of wisdom to guide us. When we are able to realize that the source of our anxiety is our thinking in the moment, our anxiety clears and makes way for insight; we return to our innate state of resiliency.

WE HAVE NO CONTROL OVER WHEN RESILIENCE WILL SHOW UP

Understanding the laws of gravity doesn't give us control over gravity, but understanding its nature allows us to live with more natural ease. In the same way, understanding the laws or Principles of how our minds work allows us to experience our innate natural resilience more readily and more often, without the intrusion of our old thoughts and beliefs.

This is a difficult concept for most of us to swallow. We like to be in control, and we see that as a strength. We have no control over when we will experience our resilience any more than we can control gravity; accepting this truth gives us a sense of awe, humility, and reverence for how human beings construct our own inner experience.

Resilience doesn't come and go; it is by nature a constant. Like gravity, it is always present. When we realize that we have made a psychological misstep, our minds clear more quickly and we learn from our mistakes. As we go through life, we often have "mini-hurricanes" even in normal times, like the birth of a child, raising an adolescent, losing a job, moving to a new location, getting a divorce, and so on. Resilience isn't just there for the big stuff of life, but for all the smaller stuff as well, as my friend Richard Carlson discussed in his book *Don't Sweat the Small Stuff*. These Principles can guide us in situations ranging from the most ordinary to the most extreme circumstances of our lives.

When the Covid-19 pandemic struck in the spring of 2020, my life was turned upside down. Due to the lockdown, I had to cancel an international conference I was hosting as well as four public speaking trips abroad. I had to begin counseling clients over Zoom instead of in person. I couldn't go to our summer cabin in Canada due to the border closing. As a very social person, I began to feel isolated from my family and friends. I had all the same human emotions as others who were going through this unfortunate experience.

Fortunately, my foundation in this understanding allowed my resilience to rise to the surface. My thinking changed, and with it, new insights sprang forth, inspiring me to reinvent my career and creatively restructure my social life. This fresh emergence of resilience empowered me to accept this crisis and embrace the opportunity to slow down, reflect, imagine, and live in a state of possibility. Out of this reflective and inspired period, this book was created.

CHAPTER SUMMARY

- Resilience is a completely natural part of life.

- We have all witnessed and experienced resilience.

- Resilience is not an action we take or an accomplishment. It surfaces naturally when our unnecessary and error-prone thinking falls away.

- We have no control over when we will experience our innate, ever-present resilience, but as we come to understand our internal barriers to it, we will see and experience it more often in our daily lives.

Ordinary Awakenings: Looking back on your life, think of a time when a solution to a problem or an insight about making a change in a job or relationship came to you, but in the moment, you brushed it off. Later, with the passage of time, you realized your intuition was trying to guide you or alert you, and you thought, "That was an insight. I should have listened to myself!"

Note: At the end of many of the chapters in this book, I will include an "Ordinary Awakenings" reflection experience. Taking the time to reflect on your own life will help bring the Principles in this book to life for you.

CHAPTER 3

THE PRINCIPLES BEHIND HOW WE EXPERIENCE LIFE

*"There was something formless and perfect
before the universe was born. It is Serene.
Empty. Solitary. Unchanging. Infinite. Eternally
present. It is the mother of the universe. For
lack of a better name, I call it the Tao."*

—Lao-tzu, *Tao Te Ching: The Book of the Way* (479 BC)

William James, founder of American psychology, once wrote that psychology had not yet become a science because its fundamental principles had not yet been discovered. He believed that this breakthrough would be revealed someday and that when it came to light, it would be the greatest discovery since the harnessing of fire. Along with many of my colleagues, I have come to believe that Sydney Banks did in fact discover these vital Principles.

Our minds are behind everything that we create—not only all our inventions, medical breakthroughs, and peace treaties, but also war, racism, violence, and destruction. Whether our creations advance or hinder the evolution of human society, all comes from the power of Mind. Unknowingly, we easily misuse this power to create our own suffering and inflict it on others.

Sydney's revelation is transforming the way we understand stress, mental illness, human relationships, and work performance within fields such as education, business, and psychology. A simple man's insight is changing the world. In these challenging times, it is paramount that we make use of our best, most insightful thinking. Only then can we solve complex issues such as pandemics, social unrest, political division, and climate change.

In this chapter, I will present these innate Principles in greater depth in the hope that this will enable readers to find freedom from fear, unleash their natural resilience, and experience their power for good.

THE LEAP OF FAITH

Earlier in my career, I used to incorporate wilderness adventures such as rock climbing and sailing into psychological growth programs. One place we liked to climb was along the cliffs of Lake Superior's North Shore. After a tiring day, we would go swimming in the Temperance River and hang onto the rocks under a waterfall to soothe our weary muscles.

We would demonstrate to program attendees that when you let go of the rock, the force of the waterfall would take you deep under the current and pop you back up to the water's surface about forty feet downstream. It was important to completely let go and trust that you would be safe. If you panicked or struggled, you might swallow some water, but eventually you would float free downstream. But no matter how logical it sounded, people would be fearful and have a hard time letting go of the rock. They learned that there was no way out except to surrender to the current and trust it to lift them to the surface due to water and fluid dynamics. Our clients grew to love this experience and wanted to repeat it every day.

It is much the same with the Three Principles. *All* principles are constants. You can always trust them to function consistently in the natural world. The new rock climbers took a leap of faith and jumped into the strong current. The moment their thoughts shifted away from fear, their innate health popped to the surface. They learned to let go of both the rock and their thoughts.

The Three Principles explain how our psychological experiences are formed. Although Syd Banks spoke of three Principles, he always said they were really one Principle with three aspects, much like the Trinity of the Father, Son, and Holy Spirit in Christianity. The Principles all work simultaneously and interdependently to form our perceptions and experiences. They are invisible forces, much like the invisible electromagnetic fields which give rise to all the atoms and molecules comprising our physical universe. I will now define each Principle before I explain how they work simultaneously to create each moment of our human experience.

MIND

The Three Principles call the Tao from the above quote "Mind." Whether we call it the Tao, Mind, The Creator, The Universal Intelligence, Brahman, The Great Nothingness or whatever else, we now know scientifically that behind visible form is a formless dance of molecules, atoms, quarks, and unseen patterns of energy.

Mind is the invisible intelligent power that acts as a catalyst to create our moment-to-moment perceptions of our existence. In Western culture, we use the words "mind" and "brain" interchangeably. This is incorrect. "Brain" refers to the physical organ in the body that acts as a human computer, storing all our memories and processing our sensory impressions so that we may experience our personal reality. "Mind," however, is the invisible intelligent power behind the brain and all life. Some would call it the "life force." When we die, the life force leaves the body and all functions of the body cease. *Mind is the life force that contains all that is known and unknown, the created and the yet to be created. Mind is the source of all insight and new knowledge that advances our personal lives and society. Insight comes to us from Mind as a thought.*

THOUGHT

Thought is the power that combines with the brain and the senses to create the personal reality we experience through perception. Thought is a constant. We are always thinking, whether consciously or unconsciously, drawing from past habitual memories, creative new thoughts, or insights. Thought is analogous to the artist's paintbrush, and our reality is analogous to the work of art. We constantly use the power of Thought to create the reality we see, whether those thoughts are positive or negative, conscious or unconscious, true or illusionary.

CONSCIOUSNESS

Consciousness is the power that brings our thoughts into experience through the senses. When Thought combines with Consciousness, we *feel* our thinking. Our senses are informed by our thoughts in the moment. Each human being is conscious of and uniquely experiences life through the lens of their personal thinking in the moment. This is why the same circumstances are met with different reactions. It isn't the circumstance that causes our feelings. It is our thoughts about the circumstance that cause our feelings. "What we see is what we get," and what we see is what we have been thinking. All experience is subjective, given that we all see "reality" based on our unique constellation of personal thoughts, beliefs, and attitudes along with our state of mind at the moment.

Consciousness is the awareness Principle. Awareness is the innate capacity to observe ourselves creating our experience. We wake up to the fact that in this moment, we are thinking and creating our personal reality. It is through Consciousness that our thoughts become our moment-to-moment sensory experience of life. Thought tells Consciousness what to see, smell, taste, touch, and hear. Consciousness makes us aware of these thoughts as an experience.

HOW MIND, THOUGHT, AND CONSCIOUSNESS COMBINE TO CREATE OUR PERSONAL REALITY OF LIFE: LEVELS OF UNDERSTANDING

Mind, Consciousness, and Thought have been the invisible powers behind every waking and sleeping moment of my life, but for almost half of my life, I had no knowledge of their existence. I was unaware of how my mind worked and didn't understand what created my sense of "reality." I was at the mercy of my thoughts, which dictated my habits, analyzed my circumstances, and formed my choices.

As I first learned about the Three Principles, they made sense on a theoretical or intellectual level, but without insight, they had no practical application to my life. However, even with my limited understanding of the Principles, they showed me a way to understand life from a new perspective and awareness. *I began to have more frequent moments where I insightfully realized that I was thinking and creating my experience and feelings from my thoughts, not from what I was thinking about.*

This realization transformed my life. I began to perceive reality in a whole new way. My burnout and stress began to disappear in a matter of weeks and lessened with each insight I had about the actual source of my experience. I gradually began to know that I was living in a reality of thought-created perceptions, sensations, feelings, and behavior.

My whole world changed and continues to change in all aspects of my life including my professional work, relationships, physical health, financial well-being, and my overall outlook on life. I started to actually experience happiness. Everything changed because my level of consciousness and understanding changed. I was *thriving* in the same circumstances where I had previously been suffering.

I didn't *make* it happen. It just happened naturally as my erroneous and unnecessary thinking fell away. It was not an action or a stress reduction technique; it wasn't something I *did*. I didn't have to *try* to be happy. My outer life gradually changed as my understanding of human experience blossomed. What I realized was that we are hardwired and perfectly designed to experience life fully. As I will show in the next section, our old habitual thinking is triggered repeatedly; and each time we have an insight, our understanding of the Principles evolves, and our level of consciousness rises. In the next chapter, I will go into more depth about this process and explain the nature of transformation and personal evolution.

THE INSIDE-OUT NATURE OF HUMAN EXPERIENCE

The Principles of human experience are guideposts on our journey through life. Most of us weren't given the driver's education manual on the workings of our mind. We were taught to keep the wheels on the road, but we didn't learn to enjoy the ride of life and be open to where it takes us. The Principles point us back to our common sense and wisdom, allowing us to weather storms, avoid obstacles, and adjust our course when we get lost or forget where we are going.

One of the essential lessons of the Principles is to *realize that we are living in an inside-out created psychological reality*. Through the Three Principles, we each create our personal reality from within our own mind. There is no absolutely direct experience of the world of form; otherwise, we would all experience outside circumstances in exactly the same way. We each experience life subjectively and create our own personal reality via the power of Thought. These three powers are the invisible forces that are creating our personal world from the cradle to the grave.

Before I met Syd Banks, I believed that my life was controlled by patterns learned as a child. I felt that these habits were stuck in me for life and believed I just needed to cope with my handicaps. It looked like other people, my past, and my circumstances were the cause of my feelings, not my thought-created perceptions of those external factors. This is the predominant current paradigm of psychological experience that I was taught as a clinical psychologist. I didn't realize that from "inside," I was connected to Mind, the source of wisdom and insight.

Now I realize that when habitual thoughts come to mind, my feelings and experience aren't coming from "out there," but from *my thoughts in the moment.* I was looking through the wrong end of the telescope. No wonder I was always bumping into things! When I began to wake up, I started seeing the real source of my feelings and perceptions of life. They were coming from my use of Mind, Thought, and Consciousness in the moment.

Now my inner observer is awake more of the time, so I am able to change my course as needed. I feel safe, secure, and comfortable in most circumstances because I have freedom to either react or not react to my thinking. The power to allow new thinking or insight and wisdom to rise to the surface effortlessly is Mind in action. We simply remove the barriers to it.

For example, recently my wife and I were driving with our boat in tow, traveling north to view the fall colors and spend a few days at my brother's lakeside cabin. On the way up, it was raining and getting dark. With the poor visibility and my unfamiliarity with the road, I saw the exit sign to the lake where his cabin is just a little late. I stepped on the brakes and skidded into the ditch. There was no way we were getting out without a tow truck. Calling wasn't an option as we were out of cell phone range, so we just waited calmly in the car for someone to come along and help. A few minutes later, someone drove up and stopped even though it was pouring rain. He helped us get the boat off the car, then went to town and called the tow service while we waited in the car, with rain still pouring down. Within forty-five minutes, we were out of the ditch and on our way to the cabin.

If this had happened in times past, our weekend would have been ruined. With our current understanding, it felt normal to stay calm and trust that things would work out. Several friendly neighbors even stopped by to see if we were okay, and we made some new acquaintances. We were amazed at how delightfully the whole event played out in the end.

WE ARE LIVING IN THE FEELING OF OUR THINKING 100 PERCENT OF THE TIME

Seeing how life and my experience of it is actually created gives me my freedom back. I am no longer a "victim" of circumstances but feel empowered and filled with hope. This understanding is the source of true security.

I often show a video in my seminars of two goldfish swimming in an aquarium. An old goldfish swims past them and says, "How's the water, boys?" The other fish look puzzled, and they turn to each other and say, "What's water?"

We are like the young goldfish, just living our lives, swimming in the water of Thought, Consciousness, and Mind. When we awaken to that psychological fact, we realize that the true source of our experience includes us as thinker and creator of our experience, no exceptions. A principle in nature has no exceptions: The sun comes up every morning and goes down in the evening, so even if it's behind a cloud, we trust that the sun is there.

At first, my understanding of the Principles was fleeting and transient. In some cases, I blamed my circumstances for my feelings; in other cases, my insight told me differently. I could see that Thought created my reaction to the weather or traffic. If my wife Michael got in a low mood, however, it seemed to me that her mood made me feel anxious or heavy, not my own thinking about her mood.

With our understanding of the Three Principles of Mind, Thought and Consciousness, we are given more freedom, patience, creativity, and compassion for ourselves and others. We respond instead of reacting, we hope instead of worrying, and we carry the knowledge that we are fine regardless of circumstances or the unknown future. With each insight into the deeper Truth of the Principles, we naturally evolve and discover the possibilities that life has to offer us.

BLIND SPOTS: MISTAKES OR OPPORTUNITIES FOR DEEPER UNDERSTANDING?

We all have blind spots—areas where we haven't yet seen the role our thinking plays. The Principles help us recognize our blind spots and understand them for what they are: parts of our lives where we haven't yet insightfully seen the role our thinking has in creating our emotional reactions.

Though I had been growing with the Principles for thirty-five years when I contracted Lyme disease, I ran into a big blind spot upon encountering that experience. The following story illustrates what this blind spot taught me.

SEEING THE POWER OF MIND IN ILLNESS

In the summer of 2017 when I had just turned sixty-nine, I noticed a drop in my overall energy level. At first, I thought my sluggishness was just caused by summer allergies. As the fatigue got worse, I began to feel aching in my finger joints but shrugged it off as arthritis due to the aging process.

Through the course of the summer, my symptoms worsened to the point where I was experiencing excruciating pain in all my joints and skeletal system, especially my spine. The impact of the physical pain was compounded by fatigue, depressed mood, and memory loss. I began to worry that I had early Alzheimer's. One night while alone at my cabin in the Canadian wilderness, I woke up in a sweat with pain more intense than I could bear. I began to wonder if it might be cancer, or perhaps a recurrence of Lyme disease, which I had experienced twice before. This time, the symptoms were different and unusual, and a visceral fear grew within me.

When I returned home, my family doctor ran a number of tests and called to say it was the worst case of Lyme he had ever seen. He immediately referred me to a specialist. Dr. V. was very knowledgeable about Lyme; having had it herself, she had found that Western allopathic medicine didn't know much about it, or how to cure it when it became chronic. To cure herself, she had gone outside the normal boundaries of medicine and through trial and error started to heal herself and many others.

She met with me for four hours, ran all kinds of tests, and spent a lot of time educating me. I changed my diet dramatically and lost thirty pounds; gradually, I felt a bit better but still not well. I continued taking forty to sixty different supplements a day and keeping a strict diet.

My mind became consumed with learning all I could about the disease. I read books, talked to my colleagues at the Mayo Clinic, searched websites, and spoke with anybody who knew anything about it. Although I was unaware of it, my mind's obsession and fear were working against my body's natural ability to heal. My doctor had said in our first meeting that my mind was the most important variable in healing from Lyme. I had agreed with her at the time but had somehow missed the depth of what she was saying. Even with all my years of experience with the Principles, I had a large blind spot.

During treatment, I cut back on my work significantly and decided to go to Malaysia with my wife, who was going to a kung fu and qigong training in Penang with a grand master. He was offering a course on qigong healing, so I decided to attend it while we were there. Before this course, we spent a week on the beaches of Thailand, sleeping, resting, and healing. We then traveled to Penang.

While my wife Michael was at her course, I decided to join her for lunch one day in Chinatown. I was hoping to meet Andrew, who was a Sifu (teacher) of qigong and a well-known healer from Switzerland. As luck would have it, I caught up with Andrew on the busy streets of Penang.

"Could I set up a time to meet with you for a session regarding my illness?" I asked.

"Let's do it now."

"Now! Here on the busy streets?"

"Why not?"

I reluctantly agreed.

"So what's the problem?"

"Well, last summer I got Lyme disease."

"Stop right there! Don't ever say you have Lyme disease if you ever want to get completely well."

Puzzled, I tried to correct him, telling him, "But I had the symptoms long before I realized I had Lyme."

With an absolute sense of knowing, he repeated what he had said earlier. "I understand the power of the mind in healing and its relationship to illness and mental health," I said. "I've written several books on that topic. I believe in what you are saying."

"No, you don't, you just *think* you do. Every time you say, 'I am sick with Lyme,' you send all the beliefs and thoughts you have about the illness to every cell of your body. Your body and mind are one."

"I know that, but…"

"Do you believe me?"

"Yes, I do, I think I do."

"No, you don't, I can see it in your face. If you don't change your thinking about your illness, your body's natural capacity to heal will be interrupted by your sending signals of being sick to the body. You don't believe me except intellectually."

I knew he was right and felt humbled by his resolve and certainty. He wasn't going to let me off the hook. At that moment, I saw it for the first time.

He smiled. "Now you believe me!"

"How do you know that?"

"I could see it in your face."

I felt something lift from my whole body—all the invisible worry and thinking was falling away. My mind swirled as it had when I had first met Syd Banks. I knew Andrew was right, but my brain kept trying to understand what had just happened.

"So, shall we set up a session?" I asked him.

"Why, we just had it?"

"That was it? But we only talked fifteen minutes at most, out here on the busy, noisy streets of Chinatown!"

"You got it, you're done."

"Well, at least let me pay your fee?"

"That's okay, don't worry about it."

The next day, I woke up early, feeling totally awake in a way I hadn't in many months, perhaps years. My head was clear, and I had all this energy. I decided to go down to the gym and work out and then go for a swim. I doubled my weights from the previous day with ease. I went for a swim and felt like I could swim forever. I didn't know what had happened, but I was grateful.

When I walked into my friend's apartment, she stared.

"What happened to you? You look ten years younger."

I told her about my conversation with Andrew the day before.

"Blake and I have been so worried about you," she said. "You had aged so much, not like before. You had always been so youthful for your age. You were our inspiration."

Andrew the healer had never heard of the Principles of Mind, Thought, and Consciousness as discovered by Sydney Banks, but he obviously had a deep understanding of Mind. My own understanding of the Principles grew immensely from my brief encounter and resulting healing after meeting Andrew.

To this day, I feel healed from that which I won't name anymore. I feel and look years younger than before I got the illness. I was not only healed from my illness, I moved to a higher level of physical, mental, and spiritual well-being. I have shared this story by video on Facebook, and it now has over ten thousand views. I am so grateful that I keep learning, evolving, and growing from the understanding of the very Principles that you are learning in this book.

CHAPTER SUMMARY

- **The Paradigm Shift:** The Three Principles represent a paradigm shift for the field of psychology in that they provide an understanding of the *fundamental principles* behind the human experience. Principles are constants that explain the fragmented and contradictory theories in this field in its present state.

- **Mind:** the invisible power that Creates our personal reality through Thought and Consciousness. Mind is the universal source of all new thinking, insight, and wisdom.

- **Thought:** the power that combines with the brain and the senses to create the personal reality we experience through perception.

- **Consciousness:** the light that illuminates our thoughts to create our personal reality; also, the capacity to be aware that we are thinking and creating our experience.

- **Levels of Understanding:** As we become more conscious of the *source* of our human experience, we experience more freedom, creativity, resilience, and well-being. We are designed for ongoing evolution and transformation.

- **The Inside-Out Nature of Experience:** We are creating our unique experience of life through our inner powers of Mind, Thought, and Consciousness, whether we know it or not. Realizing this moves our misunderstandings aside, thereby allowing the power of Mind to flow effortlessly and bring wisdom and insight into our life.

- *We are living in the feeling of our thinking 100 percent of the time.*

- **We all have blind spots:** perceived exceptions to the 100 percent truth that we are living in the feeling of our personal thinking, as in my example of Lyme disease.

PART III

THE TRANSFORMATION TO RESILIENCE: AWAKENING A NEW RENAISSANCE

CHAPTER 4

THE TRANSFORMATION PRINCIPLE

While reading the book *Illusions: The Adventures of a Reluctant Messiah* in my early twenties, I was deeply struck by one of Richard Bach's stories. His story changed my life, so I often tell my version to seminar participants and clients to help them let go of their limited views of life and see that they can trust their inner wisdom for guidance. In my version, Bach's tale goes like this:

> "Once upon a time, many creatures lived in a small village beneath the surface of a great flowing river. Like most of us, these creatures were used to their shared view of the world and didn't considered anything else. Their habit from birth was to never let go of their familiar surroundings in order to feel safe.
>
> "They'd cling to the river's banks, to the debris and the many river rocks, just to feel safe. For these creatures, clinging and resisting the flow of the rushing river was all they knew how to do.
>
> "One day one of the crayfish creatures had an idea. He announced to the village, 'I'm going to let go and see where the current takes me, for remaining here, I will surely perish of boredom.'
>
> " 'No, no, no!' everyone shouted, 'You surely will die. You'll be smashed on the rocks. No one has ever quit

clinging.' United in their shared consensus, they tried to talk him out of his dangerous idea.

"Turning away from their fears, he let go. He chose to ride the current and trust in the outcome, to see what lay beyond his village. It felt like freedom, but it wasn't always easy. Sometimes he hit the rocks, but he persisted. He saw how to go with the flow of the river. He saw a new world beyond his dreams.

"As he passed through a village downstream, the other 'clingers,' to whom he was a stranger were amazed at what they saw. 'See the miracle! It's a creature like ourselves, yet he flies! It's the Messiah coming to save us all!' "

"And the one carried in the current said, 'I am no more Messiah than you. The river delights to lift us free, if only we dare let go. Our true work is this voyage, this adventure.' "

Richard Bach, *Illusions* (1977)

OUR TRUE NATURE

We are all born free, filled with all the human potential we will ever need, guided by an impersonal intelligence called instinct, common sense, wisdom, or insight. Just hang out with a baby for a while and you will wonder at its pure innocence, curiosity, and the way it absorbs all with its keen senses. Unrestrained by fear, insecurity, and self-consciousness, young babies learn more in the first three years of life than we learn in the rest of our lives combined. They learn language as well as how to crawl, walk, run, climb, and thousands of other complex abilities.

Young children naturally express their emotions openly and get over anger or distress quite quickly. But in time, we become influenced by family and society and learn to doubt our wisdom and insights. We cling to the rocks of illusionary safety, define ourselves by our limitations, are controlled by our fears, and create our self-identity based on falsehoods. Our ego becomes a constellation of our self-defining thoughts; thus, we are unable to avail ourselves of our full potential.

However, no matter how much we cover up our innate nature and resilience, it is always just under the surface waiting for us to let go of our self-limiting beliefs and embrace who we truly are. In my work as a psychotherapist over the past forty-nine years, I have seen many miracles happen in my clients' lives. They have set themselves free of their self-limiting thoughts and uncovered their natural resilient natures. Each time this happens, their friends and family are amazed to see how they have been set free, revealing their true nature and their True Self.

In Part IV, I will illustrate the Principles behind the transformation process through people's stories. These are ordinary people from all walks of life who have begun to live extraordinary lives—drug addicts and alcoholics, stressed corporate executives, prison inmates, burned out medical professionals, first responders, parents of challenged children, victims of natural disasters, and so forth. The changes in their lives are no less than miraculous.

REMOVING THE BIG MISUNDERSTANDING REVEALS OUR NATURAL RESILIENCE

Several years ago, I was privileged to consult at the Mayo Clinic in their Heart and Lung Transplant Department as part of a four-year pilot training program on resilience. As I was walking with the department chair during rounds one day, he got a call that a heart was arriving for transplant and was coming in from New Mexico on their Lear jet. He asked if I'd like to suit up and observe him performing the operation; I jumped at the chance.

The very first thing we did was remove all our street clothes and put on scrubs. Then we began the long process of "scrubbing in." He showed me how to sterilize my hands and arms with special soap and sterile brushes—meticulously cleaning each finger, up both wrists to my elbows. I couldn't believe how long it took and how thorough he was.

As we all know now, the reason for scrubbing in and instrument sterilization is to prevent infection caused by invisible bacteria. At one time, infectious diseases were the major cause of death because germ theory didn't yet exist. When Ignaz Semmelweis discovered that bacteria were the cause of infections, he was seen as a kook and ultimately even locked up in an insane asylum due to his frustration with the medical establishment, who were resistant to his kooky ideas. Paradigm shifts are always met with resistance by the status quo. It took an entire generation for the germ theory to be adopted, which of course led to the practice of sterile techniques in medicine. Today, health experts recommend that we wear masks, wash our hands, and socially distance to prevent the spread of transmissible diseases.

Before anyone knew about germs and antiseptic procedures, well-intentioned medical professionals literally killed many of their patients. They weren't evil people. They just had an innocent misunderstanding.

Three Principles Psychology is at a similar juncture as Dr. Semmelweis was when he tried to persuade his fellow doctors to see the truth of what he had discovered.

So much of how I was trained as a clinical psychologist actually interfered with the healing process of my clients because of my own innocent misunderstanding of where the human psychological experience comes from. When I tried to share these ideas with my well-respected professional colleagues, they were skeptical and threatened by what I was sharing. As one colleague said after seeing how brief my therapy process had become and that my clients were getting well, rather than continuing therapy indefinitely, "Joe, if I change the whole way I help people, how am I going to pay for my kids' college expenses?"

The Principles reveal that our thought-created personal reality comes from the inside out. All our emotions and perceptions—what we call "reality"—is of our own making through the invisible powers of Mind, Thought, and Consciousness. Through these invisible powers, we innocently create all of our life experiences. This isn't to say there aren't significant outside circumstances, events, and other people that can influence us. How we experience what seems to be outside of us, however, is directly due to how we use these three psychological powers, whether we are aware of it or not. The possibility of returning to our resilient nature opens up once we come to insightfully realize the nature of our human experience. It's not the outside circumstances, it's how we experience them through the powers of Mind, Thought, and Consciousness.

This isn't a one-shot realization. It is a process of discernment, one insight at a time, that we call the process of transformation. After all these years, I still become hypnotized by the illusion of my personal thinking every day. But I now remind myself more quickly where my experience is coming from, and this insight reveals more of my natural resilience and all the beautiful feelings that come with it: gratitude, joy, peace of mind, love, understanding, and compassion for others.

You too will realize these Principles and the possibility of your own awakening to the truth of who and what you already are: innocent, perfect, undamaged, and whole. For some it will be a big aha experience; for others, it will be like slowly turning up the dimmer switch, as it was for me. We each have our own unique version of transformation to our True Self.

The following is a diagram which illustrates the process of first moving away from our resilient True Self, then rediscovering it anew. Some possible experiences where we move away from our insightful True Self into an egocentric belief system are seen on the downward left spiral of the diagram. The right ascending spiral illustrates possible experiences we may encounter as we wake up to our resilient True Self through transformation. This is not an exact picture of how it works; the process is usually a lot messier, but for the sake of discovery, I offer this as a reasonable facsimile.

THE SPIRALS OF EGO AND TRANSFORMATION

TRUE ESSENCE

Fear & Insecurity

Coping Mechanisms

Habits

ID with Habits

Loss of Meaning

Addiction, Unhappiness, Mental Illness, Violence

Transformation & Ongoing Evolution

ID with True Essence

Seeing Unlimited Possibilities

Seeing Thought in the Moment as Cause of My Feelings

Increased Insights

Relief, Hope

WAKING UP THRU INSIGHT
Turning Point

TRANSFORMATION TO RESILIENCE

The spiral of transformation is unique for each of us because our lives and circumstances vary. However, each of us is perfectly designed to experience transformation. I like to use the old metaphor of the caterpillar metamorphosing to become the butterfly to describe this process.

As grade school students, we were all directed to find a caterpillar and bring it to our fifth grade classroom in a jar with a perforated lid for air and a twig with a few green leaves or grass for the caterpillar's food. For the next few weeks, we impatiently watched each of our caterpillars wrap themselves in a web to form a cocoon. Some days later, they emerged as fully grown butterflies. It was miraculous and one of my most memorable learning experiences in my young school days. Science describes the process in this way:

A CATERPILLAR'S STORY OF TRANSFORMATION

Once a caterpillar sheds its skin to reveal the chrysalis that will offer protection during the process of metamorphosis, something extraordinary happens. The caterpillar starts to disintegrate! The digestive juices that used to break down its food now dissolve most of the caterpillar's body, resulting in a kind of "caterpillar soup." This creative broth contains a small number of surviving body parts as well as a huge number of imaginal cells that have been contained within the body of the caterpillar since it was born.

The imaginal cells join up to create the tissues and structures of the adult butterfly. The change from caterpillar to butterfly is not an incremental process; the caterpillar doesn't sprout wings. Rather, as the imaginal cells form together around a preexisting pattern, the butterfly emerges from the caterpillar soup.

The metamorphosis from caterpillar to butterfly can be a compelling metaphor for personal and collective transformation. The blueprint of the butterfly already exists within the body of the caterpillar, contained in the imaginal cells. Similarly, the pattern of your transformation is already there within you, contained within the eternal energy of who you really are.

The caterpillar doesn't work at becoming a butterfly; it transforms in harmony with its preexisting nature. Similarly, you don't have to struggle or work at transformation. The ability to align with your essence already exists within your nature.

We humans come into the world already equipped with the pure potential of our own transformation. All of us innocently move away from our natural True Self as we go through the uncertain and often harsh realities of our varied lives. Inevitably we develop feelings of insecurity, fear, and self-doubt and seek ways to alleviate these uncomfortable feelings. Some people become rebellious, others become perfectionistic or withdrawn. The variety of personality types and defense mechanisms has been well documented in the DSM 5 (Diagnostic and Statistical Manual). These labels are simply individual habits of thinking, not our true identity. Though many of us will never be diagnosed with a psychiatric label, we all have formed a false identity called the ego. Labels innocently force us into an identity that is not truth, but merely descriptions of our habits of thinking. At our core, we are resilient, undamaged, and whole.

THE DOWNWARD SPIRAL

The ego is not the True Essence of our being, but an innocently created false self that we have come to identify as "me." We develop various coping mechanisms to try to find our way through life. The more fear and insecurity we experience, the more destructive the habits of thinking can become, even to the point of addiction and a host of mental pathologies. However, whether our habits are diagnosable or if we are simply stressed and overwhelmed with modern life, we are all seeking a reawakening of our inner True Essence. In my book *The Serenity Principle*, I called this "the search for serenity." In *Slowing Down to the Speed of Life*, I called it "trying to find the calm in the present moment." In *Fearproof Your Life*, I referred to it as "living fearlessly." Knowingly or not, we are all searching for transformation into our True Essence.

THE UPWARD SPIRAL

The upward spiral is a guide to what the process of transformation might look like. It begins with an insight. Sometimes this insight comes from a tragic moment or period of our lives where our old coping mechanisms no longer numb the pain or alleviate our suffering. In desperation, we turn within, surrender, look for help, and admit we are lost and need an answer. Or we might become curious and seek a deeper understanding of life's true nature. Some of you in that latter category may have decided to read this book out of that deep curiosity. Others may have picked up this book at the recommendation of a friend, colleague, or a counselor, in order to find your way "back home."

It takes a degree of willingness, humility, and openness to begin the journey upward. Whether the motivation is born of curiosity or arises out of suffering and desperation, it matters not. Once you recognize that your ego is looking in the wrong direction through faulty thinking, you are on the trajectory of transformation. This is usually accompanied by a feeling of hope and relief and a sense of clarity and resolve.

The Three Principles are an aid to this process. I have worked with addictions for over forty-eight years, and before I discovered the Principles, my therapeutic successes were limited and effortful. I now have a quicker and less painful way to help others find themselves on the transformation side of this diagram and begin the ongoing process of evolution and transformation. Once we see the big misunderstanding of where our experience and feelings are coming from, our erroneous and unnecessary egocentric thinking begins to fall away. We experience the deeper, more gratifying, natural feelings of our True Self.

The spiral is not a straight line of change. Rather, at times we seem to be going backward or getting stuck on the hamster wheel of habitual thinking. That happens to me on a regular basis. But sooner or later, our wisdom kicks in and we remember the origin of our negative feelings, *not from what we are thinking about, but from our response to these thoughts.* Once we truly become aware of the sole source of our psychological experience, this "seeing" will stick with us for the rest of our lives. We experience a sense of humility, relief, and gratitude for this insight. It is all so simple, like wearing a mask or washing our hands to prevent disease. But in this case, we wash clear our misunderstandings of thought to prevent disease of the mind.

With a great sense of mental clarity, hope, and openness, we see unlimited possibilities. It is like getting personally unstuck. We make better decisions and take right actions in accord with those decisions, creating a healthier and more harmonious workplace and community. There is no end to transformation, and I can assure you it only gets better, even though at times it can appear we are losing it at the point we call "the darkest hour just before the dawn."

Now we will take a deeper look at the process of what happens in the "loops" as we move up the spiral of transformation. Within the ongoing evolution of our consciousness, we often appear to have lost what we thought we knew as we slip back into old thinking patterns and fall prey to our blind spots. This is actually not a failure or a setback, but an opportunity for increased insight and realization. When we understand the process of transformation more deeply, we welcome "setbacks" or "slips" as an opportunity to gain deeper understanding.

Here is a magnification of one of the loops in the ongoing transformation process:

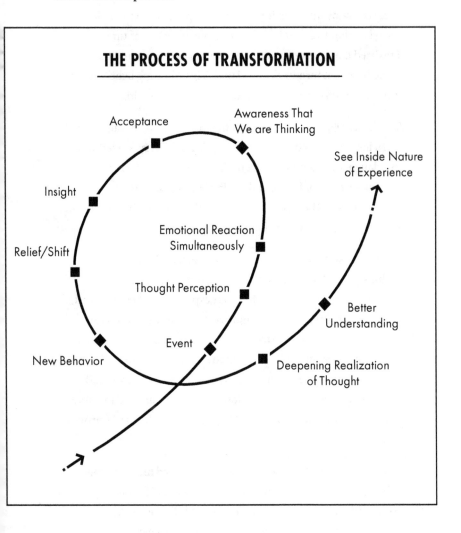

THE PROCESS OF TRANSFORMATION

Early on in my introduction to the Principles, I used to think, "Maybe I don't get this," or, "Is this really true?" Over time, I realized that the way we discover a blind spot is to run into something that throws us off balance. This "flashing light" is built into the design of the natural process of transformation.

Toddlers are quite unstable when they are learning to walk and will often lose their balance and fall. Sometimes they cry, sometimes they laugh, but they always get back up and try again. Over time, after many trials of falling and getting back up, they eventually stay upright most of the time. Even adults still occasionally fall, but since we *know* we can walk, we don't doubt our ability.

As we are psychologically evolving, we fall back into old habits of thinking and behaving from time to time. However, with an understanding of how and where our experience is being created, our learning curve begins to improve dramatically. As you can see from the diagram, the trajectory of transformation is upward even though we often hit bumps in the road. We might wake up in a low mood, or our mate says something that triggers old defensive thinking patterns, we lose our job, or our child throws a temper tantrum—the "small and big stuff" of life Richard Carlson wrote about.

When we hit a wall from one of life's unexpected moments, our habitual ego-based thought system is activated; old thought patterns and emotional responses become triggered. This is totally normal and is part of the maturation process. When we begin to see these "setbacks" or "bumps in the road" not as failures or as proof "this doesn't work," but *as opportunities for deeper understanding,*

our bumps transform into deeper insights into the nature of
the Principles.

Insights occur quite naturally as I become aware that my emotional
reactions aren't coming from "what I am thinking about, but the
fact that I am thinking." This is not an intellectual insight derived
from analyzing and postulating. Trying hard to figure things out
slows down the process of insight. It is a "gentle awareness," a
glimpse of seeing where my experience is coming from.

LIFE HAPPENS AND SOMETIMES TRIGGERS HABITUAL THINKING

Each challenge we face in life can trigger illusionary, habitual
thinking. When this happens, it appears as though "this one event"
is an exception to the Principles, but this is not true. There are no
exceptions to a Principle. We really do not have control over old
insecure and fearful thoughts that enter our minds. When such
thoughts are activated, we simultaneously experience an emotion
which is really just a sensory experience of that thought: *We feel our
thinking.* Thought is very deceptive in that it immediately creates
an illusion which Consciousness brings to life. We may innocently
believe that this event is an exception to the 100 percent Principle of
how our reality is always created by our thoughts and relapse into
the illusions of our ego-based thought systems and beliefs.

WE LIVE IN THE FEELING OF OUR THINKING

We can only ever experience our thinking in the moment.
Sometimes that fact appears to have exceptions, as with our
illusionary thinking that our mood revolves around our
child's mood. However, it is quite human to be fooled by this

illusion. When this happens, old familiar feelings of fear, anger, powerlessness, and worry come back to haunt us. We retreat into our old automatic conditioned responses, which is another way of describing our habits. No matter what technique we try, we have no control over what thoughts suddenly appear. And the beauty of this understanding is that it doesn't matter.

For example, a client recently shared this story:

> "I thought I was doing so well after treatment, which included learning about the Three Principles. I felt so much more peace of mind and was seemingly able to roll with the punches. Then one day after a disappointing performance at my music gig, I became really down. I was used to playing with a few beers and didn't know if I could perform as well without the alcohol boost in my newfound sobriety. The next day, my wife questioned whether I had really changed or not. This was her old insecure thinking talking. My old habitual thinking came rushing in, and I withdrew into angry and defensive feelings.

> "Then, in a moment of insight, I saw that my feelings had nothing to do with her reaction or my performance the night before, but solely related to my thinking in the moment. This realization woke me up and my emotions immediately shifted. I felt humbled by how quickly I could lose my bearings and grateful that I had caught it in time, averting a major blowout with my wife and a potential relapse into drinking. Life gave me this opportunity to gain more understanding, and my confidence soared with the power of knowing the source of my experience."

What my client came to was a simple shift in his Consciousness of where his experience was originating, not from outside circumstances but from the power of Thought itself. With this awareness, and without effort, his feelings shifted from defensiveness, anger, disappointment in himself, and lowered confidence to gratitude, relief, forgiveness, and compassion toward himself and his wife. From that moment onward, every time he lost his bearings, he graciously took it as a chance to shift to a higher level of understanding. Instead of being held hostage by his feelings, he became excited about new inner discoveries.

This is the game of life, one that is a little like the game of hide-and-go-seek. When we lose the feelings of inner peace, joy, and gratitude that come with living from the inside, it is simply an opportunity for us to go seek a deeper insight into the nature of reality.

When it appears that our true identity is "hiding," we are in a moment of recognition that our thinking may be off. Rather than reverting back to old habitual thinking and insecurity, we can open our minds to new thinking. When life hands us an opportunity disguised as a problem, we point ourselves in the direction of new discovery, constant evolution, and transformation and wait for insight to arrive—and arrive it does.

THE WISDOM OF INSECURITY

ASKING REAL QUESTIONS: OUR INNER SEARCH ENGINE

Each time we encounter a setback, a fork in the road, or a challenge that seems overwhelming, an insightful question will usually come to our mind. "Why is this happening to me? What do I need to learn from this experience? Is there something I'm not seeing here?"

These are inspired questions. They open our minds to receive new insights—not by trying to figure it out with our intellect. This is our built-in Google to the Universal Mind.

When we realize that we can absolutely trust in our inner wisdom to guide us, boatloads of insecure thinking fall away, and we feel a sense of deep security and calm. When we understand that what's happening is a "thought experience" about life, not life doing it *to* us, we return to the quiet center in the eye of the hurricane. That is when a new thought or insight pops into our minds, seemingly from out of the blue.

Here are some insights that may occur as our minds quiet down:

- A *problem* can be seen as an *opportunity* for new and deeper insight. If action is required, the step-by-step solution will come to us.

- We accept what we're feeling and perceiving without judgment. We *accept our own humanity.*

- We're willing to *open ourselves to new thinking.* We learn to trust that insight will come as needed.

- Our tendency to judge ourselves and others begins to fade away. We are *not as interested in analyzing* or trying to figure out *why* this is happening.

- We see the importance of continually *pointing ourselves toward inner understanding* by simply being aware that we are having a thought created experience.

- When confused, *we turn to our true selves for answers*—the Google within.

- *We can't control when insight will arrive,* but we can stop getting in the way. As we connect again with the essence of who we are, willingness, openness, and humility begin to appear, and we move deeper and deeper into our wisdom.

When I first learned the Principles forty-one years ago, I was very anxious, stressed, and burned out. In spite of my initial insights on how reality is being created, I quickly returned to my chaotic life. Each time I fell back into my old habits, it would eventually dawn on me, "My schedule or challenging day isn't stressing me, it's my *thinking* about this day that is stressing me. I created the schedule, and I can change it, too."

The simplicity of this truth would hit me, and then I would relax. My perception of the day would shift, and everything would smooth out. Each time I fell back into my old, habitual, stressful thinking, I would be brought back to a deeper insight. Eventually, my burnout left, and my stress-provoking clients no longer bothered me at all. As I changed within, my outside world appeared to change as well.

For the past forty-one years, this has been my life:

- I react to something in an unhealthy way.

- I feel emotionally imbalanced.

- I remember who is creating my experience.

- My feelings and my perception shift with this awareness.

- I gain deeper insight into how my experience of life is actually created.

Although I still relapse back to habitual thinking, with my growing understanding, the trajectory is no longer a downward spiral of hamster wheel thinking. Now it is a trajectory of insight, evolution, and built-in self-correction. That can happen for you and for all of us once we see how life actually works to create our unique experience.

This simple logic eluded me (and most of humanity) for eons. Our lives don't change until our thinking changes and slowly spirals upwards with increasing insight. This is the process of transformation. Life becomes more of an adventure than just a struggle for survival. Onward and upward!

In the next chapters, I will provide stories to illustrate the process of transformation that results from the Principles. Real-life stories will help you get a feel for the process and demystify it.

I would like to share my wife's beautiful poem which illuminates this awakening.

THE CHRYSALIS OPENS

Achieving unity with "Now" is a powerful force.
Achieving unity with "Now" is a powerful source.

Reflection has greatness. Reflection is profound,
showing you the edge where the world turns around.

Creation is a power available to use,
open and willing to work for you.

Openings come when we look inside,
our mind expands seeing everything wide.
Expand, Expand…

I've come to talk of you and Me, we're the same
and the source of everything to see.

The chrysalis is designed for you to be Me,
this pathway is open for you to be free,
Fly butterfly, fly away from the past,

it's time to move on for you to surpass
any considerations, concerns or loss,

your life is your future, reclaim you as whole,
all that you are and never did know,

your wings are salvation for you to find
what's hidden within you, never left behind.

The chrysalis dissolves and you will fly through the air,
no longer fearing what is out there.

You dreamed you could fly freely,
now you are ready to soar,
your wings are designed to show you more…

Possibilities unlimited, explorations divine,
the world is yours to create and design.

Create a new world designed from your heart,
created from love, we won't be apart.

Fly butterfly fly

—Michael Bailey © 10/2020

PART IV

ECHOES OF MIND: RESILIENCE IN ACTION

The stories in the following chapters showcase people from all walks of life. I have organized them thematically to enhance readers' understanding of the Principles. Though the stories vary greatly, I ask you to look for the common thread of resilience and insight that has helped each of these individuals to thrive, no matter what their unique challenges were. Stories often have the power to touch us more deeply than words that do not involve a narrative; they can give us hope, provide direction, trigger insight, and inspire us to begin the journey of transformation into infinite possibility.

Here are three fundamental points to notice that run through each life story and show the wisdom that lies within us all:

- *We are all innately resilient,* no exceptions; we are never broken, never damaged.

- *We all create our unique personal reality from the Principles of Mind, Consciousness, and Thought from within us.* That is our power to either use wisely or innocently misuse.

- *We are all connected to Mind, a constant that guides us through life* by means of the inner voice of insight, wisdom, and common sense. It is a constant that we can count on to bring us back to resilience.

CHAPTER 5

THRIVING IN THE UNKNOWN: HOPE SPRINGS ETERNAL

*"For years I tried to extinguish the light inside of me
Not knowing it was my spirit trying to burn brightly
Now my spirit lights up the world from where I stand
Once a lost, empty, lonely man*

*"Now a beacon of hope and inspiration for others to
see my light and help guide them to their true spirit
Once where my heart was so black
Like a piece of coal on a cold fire*

*"Now so full of love my heart glows a richness of all
that's good
I feel the life run through my veins
The same ones I tried so hard to tether*

*"My heart my soul so full of joy and peace and love
I now feel at home."*

—Peter Mears

Peter discovered the Principles in the UK through a program called
Beyond Recovery. He struggled with alcoholism much of his life

and lost so much, but nothing was really lost, only hidden from him through his innocent misunderstanding of who he really was and of the Principles creating his experience of life. Now free, he shares what he knows to help others discover their resilience and innate mental health.

We are perpetually walking into the "unknown." You may wonder why the so-called "unknown" is important to understand. When we know the Principles of how life functions, we can see how these same Principles apply to our daily lives as well. We aren't tempted to make up things about what *might* happen next. We can relax with the understanding that life is a moment-to-moment experience— one thought, one perception, one feeling, one experience at a time. We cannot know the future, for it does not yet exist.

Many think that constantly engaging in intellectual strategizing will protect us, or that by rehashing the past, we'll experience closure. That misconception only leads us to innocently slip into a misuse of the Principles. We begin to create scenarios, often based on our deepest fears of what may come next. When we churn thoughts of the future in our minds based on beliefs rather than wisdom, we create feelings of fear, worry, dread, anxiety, anticipation, and hopelessness, to name a few.

For years before we met, one client of mine read and listened to self-help audios in which the "unknown" was mentioned frequently. She was very familiar with the term and was convinced she had an accurate understanding of it. As I listened to her, it became apparent she was only focusing on an intellectual concept, and that the concept was terrifying her. Her thoughts about what the unknown meant resurrected fears from old traumas and triggered her habit of running to her intellect to create a plan for future protection, which never worked.

She knew the Principles and had insights about the Principle of Thought, but her propensity to jump into the future was still a blind spot. She was becoming more able to see the difference between thoughts and insights coming from Universal Mind and experiences coming from an intellectual tirade of thoughts and beliefs about life.

I was able to help her see the difference between her concept about the unknown with the truth of what the unknown really is. It was wonderful to watch her face relax and her eyes come alive when she directly experienced what the term "the unknown" really meant. It was not a scary mystery anymore. She was relieved to see the truth of how life and creation work. She easily agreed that of course the future is unknown since it's in a perpetual state of flux. At the end of that session, she decided she preferred the idea that "the unknown" was better understood as *endless possibilities.*

Once we gain an insightful understanding of how the human experience is created, we will continue to more deeply see that we are built for resilience and transformation. We realize that we can trust the Principles to give us new thoughts in the form of insights, creative solutions, possibilities, and answers to questions we've never thought of before. Trusting in the wisdom that Sydney Banks speaks of is our birthright; it shows us how to adapt and find solutions to the changes in our world, including how to deal with Covid-19, how to raise our children who are homebound, how to make a living, and how to go fearlessly into the unknown. The next story from an earlier time during World War II will help illustrate how love and hope help us thrive in a "hopeless" situation.

HOPE SPRINGS ETERNAL: THRIVING IN A PRISON CAMP

Forty years ago, I met Dr. George Ritchie, who was one of the soldiers who went into the prison camps in Nazi Germany at the end of World War II to rescue survivors and reunite them with their families. I was in a fellowship program to become a Three Principles practitioner; he was attending the program as well. He became a psychiatrist after the war and spent his life trying to help others realize the remarkable resilience he saw in some of the survivors.

He was amazed anyone could possibly survive the conditions the Jewish prisoners had experienced—starvation, beatings, the horrors of the extinction ovens, and separation from their loved ones, with no hope of escape. Yet some prisoners, even after years in Auschwitz and other camps, were resilient, hope-filled, and engaged in loving service to others. How could they remain resilient in the face of those conditions? He said the Three Principles were the first breakthrough that could explain how this was possible.

He told my wife Michael and I a story about a man he'd named "Wild Bill" because of his long handlebar mustache. Wild Bill was one of the few prisoners who looked vibrant, hopeful, and energetic when George arrived at the camps. Puzzled, Dr. Ritchie asked him if he had just arrived. Bill responded that he had been there for five years. In disbelief, Dr. Ritchie asked Bill to explain how he had not only survived these horrific conditions but had apparently *thrived through them.* Bill shared his story of having witnessed the Germans coming into his small Jewish village and killing everyone he had ever known—his family, friends, and acquaintances—in front of him. His heart was filled with hatred for the Germans as he plotted revenge.

Then he'd had an insight, one which he shared with us.

"If I hate and kill them, I am no better than those who were my persecutors. I vowed that day to only live in love. Love kept me alive." Over those five years, he never lost his hope of reconnecting with his remaining relatives. He spread hope, humor, and love to all with whom he came into contact. Dr. Ritchie shared that Bill looked healthy, joyful, and full of life. Somehow, through his insight, he had touched Mind—the source of all unconditional love, hope, joy—all the deeper feelings that humanity seeks.

The secret to thriving in the unknown is experiencing the feeling of hope. Hope isn't something conditional based on some particular event in the future we hope will happen. Hope is not attached to an outcome. Hope is a feeling that is part of who we are in our True Self, the Essence of all things.

False hope is tied to an outcome: "I'll be happy when I finally get a job." "I'll be happy when this pandemic is over and we can get back to normal." That is conditional hope, and it usually gives us a momentary feeling of hope, but this is not true hope, and it quickly fades into fear of the unknown.

CONDITIONAL HOPE	HOPE FROM INSIDE
Imagining positive scenarios	Knowing there are infinite possibilities
From ego/habits	From our True Self
Momentary relief	A constant knowing
Controlling	Trusting in Wisdom of Mind
Results: fear, worry, effort, stress, limited possibilities	Results: peace of mind, insights, creative solutions

True hope is unconditional and is a natural part of resilience. When we finally feel true hope, our mind is open to seeing unlimited possibilities that lie before us, even if it was previously blinded by our ego-based thinking.

This next story centers on inmates in the UK who were addicts and learned about the Principles while in prison. It clearly illustrates the power of resilience and true hope.

HOPE INSIDE: A NEW BEGINNING AFTER A LIFE OF CRIME AND ADDICTION

Jacqueline Hollows is the founder of Beyond Recovery, a program in the UK prison system to help inmates find true recovery from addictions, trauma, and destructive behavior and begin life anew. Her program began with an inspired idea. After her own pain and recovery, she started working with people with addictions, and through the despair and crime in their lives, she could see hope and resilience. She had the thought, "I really want to help those people." Though she had no experience with inmates or treatment, she just felt a powerful inner urge to help this population and bring them hope.

Little by little, her dream came true; she started her Beyond Recovery program, which eventually spread to several prisons around the UK. She had started out with no idea how to help the inmates, but she had trusted her innate wisdom to guide her on each step of the journey.

When I asked how and why she was able to do this, she said, "I consider myself to be a talent scout, discovering so much unrealized potential in these souls in prison and helping them to see who they really are." Although there were many, many obstacles, she was "discouragement proof" and never gave up on the prison system or on the inmates.

As one of her "Beyond Recovery Boys" (whom I will call "James" for the purpose of this story) put it:

> "My hope began with Jacqueline seeing hope in me. She never gave up on me. She saw something in me I didn't see in myself. No matter how many times I screwed up, she never lost hope in me. That ignited my own spark of hope, which began to surface from within. My resilience, my True Self began to make itself known. That feeling of hope is my True Self, and from there I have an endless supply of insight into limitless possibility. Over time while in prison the whole way I related to my fellow prisoners, to my wife and children, and to the guards changed. Now I am out of prison and have started a program for the families of inmates called "Beyond Truth" and see hope for everyone I meet. I had to go to prison to find true freedom, go figure!"

When James was first realizing the Principles while in prison, one day, he was waiting for his wife and young son to come for a visit. She was forty-five minutes late, which was not unusual, but he became agitated as he saw all the other prisoners laughing and talking with their love ones. He imagined they were all staring and making fun of him as he squirmed in the corner, his embarrassment and anger growing.

Then, he told me, "I had an insight and realized that my wife is always late. She has two young children to get ready for the trip, and she has to drive sixty miles to visit me. She must love me to go to all that trouble."

He asked the guard to call her; and sure enough, she was on her way and would be there shortly. When she arrived, instead of being angry and having another typical argument, he was full of love for her and felt gratitude for being able to see his children. She was feeling rushed and guilty and expected James to be angry, and she didn't quite know what to say or how to respond. She got defensive, but he didn't react and instead just stayed calm and loving. Eventually, she calmed down and they had a beautiful visit.

The realization that his feelings were coming from past memories and habits allowed his wisdom and love to surface. He said, "I realized 'it takes two to tango,' " explaining he'd become aware that if he didn't react to her reaction out of habit, he could remain calm, and that eventually, she would calm down too.

Now James is out of prison, and though they are divorced, he has the best relationship with her he has ever had, and this has allowed him to be the dad he always wanted to be.

Let us revisit the diagram from chapter 3 so we can track the process of James's transformational experience. The event was his wife being late for a visit while he was in prison. He perceived this as her not loving or respecting him. This led to feelings of hurt, anger, and embarrassment about what the other prisoners were thinking about him. Then he had a moment of clarity—an insight—where he saw that his feelings were coming from a misuse of his power of thought, not from his wife. Upon realizing that, he felt relief and began to perceive his circumstances in a new light. With that insight, his typical behavior changed, and instead of greeting her with anger and a sulking demeanor, he felt unconditional love for his wife and the kids. Even though she didn't come around in an emotional sense for a while, his wisdom and resilience protected him from her reactions, and this led to a change in their relationship. Each time he had a similar insight, his level of understanding about the true nature of the human experience rose. With his rise in understanding, the quality of his life dramatically changed; first, when he began working as a counselor in the prison, then with eventual release from prison into a new life. He has now spoken to large groups at conferences in many parts of the world.

James's story is only one of hundreds of similar stories of transformation happening not only in this program in the UK, but in other prisons in California, Oregon, and Minnesota, to name a few. In one of the California prisons where these Principles have been taught, a group of inmates were on death row awaiting execution. One inmate from this group said in an interview, "I never thought I would experience true freedom while in prison, knowing I would never be released from death row. Now I am truly free."

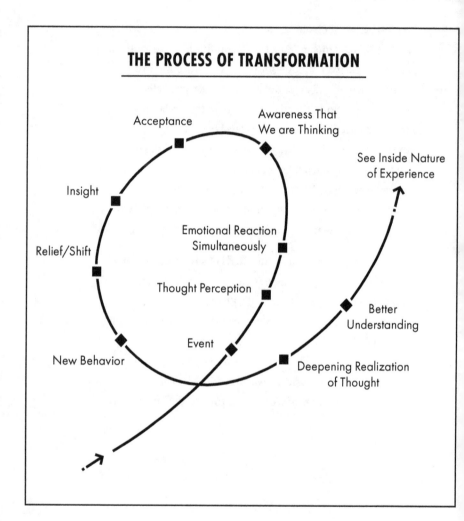

THE PROCESS OF TRANSFORMATION

GRACEFUL GRIEF: DEALING WITH LOSS

"I met Francesco in a moment of fate when I sat next to him on a plane from London to southern Italy fourteen years ago. Coincidently, we ended up on the same flight going back to London at the end of our vacation. We fell in love and became partners. Eventually, we both decided to leave London and went back to Italy to live permanently.

"Six years ago, I attended a Michael Neill retreat in Barcelona, Spain, and discovered the Three Principles. It changed my stressful life to one of true peace of mind. Originally, I was looking for even more success in my coaching practice, but what really changed was that Francesco's and my relationship grew even deeper in love with my newfound understanding. For the last five years of his life, we had a much richer and deeper love than we had before. Prior to discovering the Principles, I had a hesitancy about the relationship. After that, I was all in. We lived an idyllic life.

"Then two months ago, without warning, my love Francesco suddenly died at age forty-five. He was healthy and in good shape. I ran into him on the street just prior to his death as I was on the way to have a cappuccino with my friend. We waved and said hi as I was going down the street at the moment when he drove by. I never dreamed that would be our last moment together.

"When I arrived home, Francesco was lying there dead, keeled over on the bed. He had a preexisting condition that his grandfather and uncle had died of as well. When I saw him lying there, I surprisingly felt the deepest love I had ever experienced with him up to that point. I was shocked that I felt this overpowering feeling of love.

"I now see loss as a doorway to love. My love for him transcends my grief. I still feel the whole gamut of emotions, which I completely accept and experience. They flow through me and move on. Then what's left is just the love. Sometimes it amazes me the strength of this love that's available even though he's now gone. Then some days I feel the loss, the regret, the pain, but I don't get stuck there. It passes through naturally, and then the love comes back.

"Going through grief without fear is how I'd describe this experience. It means going through grief without a second layer of suffering. I am grateful to know what I know. It feels like a bubble of protection, especially when I'm low. While listening to a speaker share his sister's traumatic experience when her fiancé died the night before their wedding, I realized what my experience of Francesco's death could have been like. Without our spiritual heritage, the Principles, I wouldn't know where the source of all experience comes from. Instead, I would be deeply afraid of my experience and suffer greatly.

" 'Surely death is the exception to the rule?' I asked; 'Surely in losing the love of your life there can't be good days, state of mind can't play any role?' Not true. Death is not the exception. I have terrible days, but in those hours or days, I'm not afraid of my experience. I know that the storm will pass, and when it does, I'm back to feeling blessed and comforted by the evidence of Francesco's eternal love and spirit living on. Unlike the speaker's sister, I'm not afraid of this experience. That second layer of suffering isn't hooking me and getting me into a collapse or a terrible fear of my future. It is grief with a level of grace. It is loss with an undercurrent of resiliency. It is tragedy with a sense of eternal love, the love that never dies. Who knew this was possible? Death is not the exception. My love is more complete now even in his death. Now I know that I loved and was truly loved. Love doesn't have to die with death. All the resistance is gone to my love for him. My understanding of the Principles and his death led to a deeper understanding of Mind. I was surrounded by a deep feeling of love. The physical was not important to me anymore. I felt love everywhere, protecting me, guiding me. I wasn't afraid. I had deep knowing that he and I were both okay—that we had both loved each other deeply and are continuing to. It was a deep experience of Mind. Nothing compares to that feeling of love.

"If I didn't understand how my experience is created through the Three Principles moment to moment, I would be having much more suffering in my grief process. I am not afraid of the feelings of sadness, regret, anger, ruminating. Now I just see them for what they are: a thought in the moment. Seeing that takes me back to the moment and to the love I have and still get to experience in my love for him. This experience of his death pulled me into the present moment, the source of all well-being and true love."

The previous stories present us with the idea that no matter how tragic, how painful, or how hopeless our lives have become, there is always the possibility that we can still find our resilience, hope, and peace of mind. Each story is unique—from a life of alcohol addiction to being in a Nazi prison camp, and from being in a gang and a drug addict in prison to suddenly losing the love of your life to death.

Each of these people's experiences demonstrates the resilient nature of the human spirit, and with an understanding of the Principles, aids us in recovering our true essence, and with it, a beautiful life.

Ordinary Awakenings: Reflect on your own life for a moment, given that we are all living in the unknown future of endless possibilities. How might you see a past disappointment, hurt, or failure through the lens of your resilience and the insightful power of thought?

CHAPTER 6

WHY HOPE AND RESILIENCE ARE THE KEY TO THE MIND/ BODY CONNECTION IN DEALING WITH ILLNESS

Earlier, in chapter three, I shared my story of healing from Lyme disease and my profound realization of the role that my invisible thinking played in preventing my body's natural ability to heal my symptoms. After my healing experience, I was contacted by a colleague specializing in healing who asked me to do a webinar series on "The Healing Power of Mind." We had over forty participants with a variety of conditions, illnesses, and chronic diseases. By sharing the Principles with them and helping them see the mind/body connection, many people were either healed or their suffering was lessened.

It is common sense that our attitude toward illness is an important factor in the healing process. Norman Cousin's 1979 book *Anatomy of an Illness* was the first popular book that pointed to the power of the patient's attitude in the healing process, both through humor and the patient participating in healing from their cancer. Later, oncologist Dr. Bernie Siegel wrote *Love, Medicine and Miracles* about the power of the mind in the healing process. (Dr. Siegel also wrote an endorsement for my book *Slowing Down to the Speed of Life*.) Their ideas began a movement in medicine to humanize the treatment process and provide medical education that emphasized the healing power of the mind.

Years ago when I was doing the Inner Life of Healers Program at the University of Minnesota School of Medicine, I visited with Earl Bakken, inventor of the pacemaker and founder of Medtronics Corporation. His foundation was one of our funders, and I met with him in Hawaii to explore doing retreats at his hospital on the Big Island. He shared how he had become interested in the mind/body connection and the importance of the state of mind of the physician in the healing process. He shared that in researching all the variables correlated with pacemaker rejection, one puzzling anomaly kept coming up: the bedside manner or state of mind of the surgeon implanting the device. As a scientist, he couldn't ignore this factor and became very interested in how medical schools could encourage the health of the helper, whether physicians, nurses, or other healthcare providers.

In chapter 9, I will discuss how the attitude of the physician in the healing process and the attitude of the patient toward their treatment both strongly influence the treatment outcome. We'll go in depth about the Principles' positive impact on doctors, nurses, and other healthcare professionals, facilitating their becoming more resilient and more impactful with their patients. In this chapter, I will share powerful stories of how the Principles have helped people who are suffering from chronic illness or assisted people in dying more peacefully.

CHRONIC PAIN AND CHRONIC FATIGUE MINUS THE SUFFERING

Chana had been mugged three times; as a result, she suffered chronic pain from her major injuries. For twenty-five years, she had been seeing a chiropractor weekly to cope with her pain. She also pursued many self-development courses such as the Enneagram and A Course in Miracles, knowing that her psychological health would be a key factor in coping with the chronic pain. She became highly vigilant about her thoughts in regard to her PTSD and tried to stay positive using numerous techniques and strategies. At the time, she hadn't yet realized that all her unnecessary thinking was triggering her fight-or-flight response and weakening her body's immune system and its natural ability to heal itself. This misunderstanding was totally innocent on her part. She even became a coach to help others deal with their chronic pain prior to her breakthrough in understanding how her experience was being created.

Six years ago, Chana learned about Three Principles Psychology and realized why her thinking was connected to her hypervigilance and her chronic pain. Pursuing all these techniques and trying to think positively were actually exacerbating her pain. She was always trying to do gratitude exercises, affirmations, and other survival techniques, but this only resulted in more hypervigilant thinking. This in turn sent signals throughout her body keeping her in fear and thus undermining her healing.

This was the same lesson I referred to earlier in this book in my story of healing from Lyme disease. My blind spot as a Three Principles counselor and teacher was the same as Chana's, in the sense that I didn't see the connection between my chronic thinking about Lyme and my inability to experience healing. Chana eventually realized her innocent misunderstanding of the role her thinking had been playing in keeping her pain active. She didn't *do* anything, she just began to identify with her True Essence or Mind, which, when experienced, does all the healing. When we trust in the river to carry us down the stream, we are guided back to health.

This doesn't necessarily mean we are "cured" of a disease, although we might be, but rather that we no longer needlessly suffer because of our thinking about this disease. Mind guides us through insight to do what we might need to do on a physical level to help alleviate our pain or to heal, without all the unnecessary thinking about the condition that creates the actual suffering and stresses the body's immune system. This is the mind/body connection.

Chana has just written a book about her experience called *Painless*. (Please see recommended resources at the end of this book for publication information.)

JOHN'S STORY OF CHRONIC FATIGUE

"Do you know how much energy it takes for you to be this tired?"

These were the words uttered by John's functional medicine doctor, words that finally cemented John's understanding of why he had been sick for so long.

For seven years, John had been severely debilitated with chronic fatigue syndrome, which at his worst had left him hospitalized and bedbound for three months. For years, he suffered from a myriad of symptoms, including crippling fatigue and tiredness, anxiety, diffuse pain, digestive symptoms, dizziness, and sensitivity to light and sound. One of the symptoms that he found hardest to contend with was heat and sunlight intolerance. Exposure to either for even short periods could leave him feeling faint and nauseous and would typically end in a headache and a sense that his skin was burning within moments. Coping with this required him to take cold showers, sleep without bedcovers at times, and "shadow walk" in the shade of buildings so that he could avoid exposure to the sun. The latter was particularly distressing for him as he really wanted to be able to play with his young kids outside.

Before his breakthrough insight, John had all but given up on ever making a full recovery. He had little hope until the words of his doctor finally came together with his growing understanding of the Three Principles. He saw that his driven nature as a high achiever and an over-planner had resulted in his trying to control life with his intellectual mind. It was constantly revving up his thinking. His invisible thinking was telling his nervous system that he was not safe and that it needed to remain in a constant state of fight-or-flight. When he became sick, this tendency became worse; he found himself constantly thinking about his symptoms, tracking whether they were improving or worsening, and wondering how he was going to cope with his life.

John, like many of us, innocently failed to understand the Principle of Mind and the Universal design that affects all aspects of life. Prior to becoming sick, he had lived his life unaware of the body's intelligence and the multitude of processes and chemical reactions that functioned even without him knowing or thinking about them. He didn't realize that this intelligence had always been there in every area of his life as a quiet knowing guiding him to make decisions, create ideas, and navigate challenges. It had always seemed like his intellectual thinking was doing the heavy lifting of his life.

But his doctor's words made it all click. John's symptoms were real, but they were not being caused by some horrible undiagnosed pathology. They had arisen through John's innocent misunderstanding of the Three Principles. The more he tried to be well by constantly figuring out and trying to troubleshoot his life and his illness, the more his body was activated into a state of breakdown and the more his symptoms and his energy spiraled downwards.

When the penny dropped for John, change came about quickly. What had been a seven-year journey of suffering turned around in a matter of weeks. His insight helped him to understand the nature of his symptoms and fired him from the job of managing both his life and his illness. There was a new sense that if there was something he needed to do, like go to the doctor or make a decision, it would come from the quiet knowingness of Mind, and there was a feeling that it was actually safe for him not to think too much.

The more John dropped out of vigilant thinking, the more his body relaxed and his symptoms abated. The ultimate reward was being able to go on a summer holiday with his family just two months after his insight. His symptoms were gone, and he was freed from having to "shadow walk" to avoid the light of the sun. Finally, he was able to go to the beach and play outside with his kids—a very big moment for him.

John's journey eventually led him to begin helping others suffering from chronic fatigue. Starting out first by sharing the Principles with other individuals and friends dealing with chronic fatigue, he eventually moved to conduct a peer-reviewed research study to test the efficacy of the approach more formally. It was the first such study to test the efficacy of the Three Principles in helping people with physical illness.

The results of this study were published by the American Psychological Association (APA) and were described by the editor as "groundbreaking." The data showed statistically significant improvements in measures for fatigue, well-being, anxiety, depression, and pain. Some of the results were startling, including benefits to individuals who had been unwell for nearly twenty years and were finally able to break free of their fatigue condition. One individual, who was confined to moving around in a wheelchair because he was so weakened by his condition, was finally able to let it go; he improved dramatically and is now living his life normally. Along with this, individuals taking part in the study also reported anecdotal improvements in comorbidities such as food intolerances and allergies, chronic pain, and other autoimmune disorders like psoriasis and immunodeficiency.

Although the study size was small and further research is needed, the study's results provide hope that working with the Principles might have positive effects on other illnesses in addition to chronic fatigue syndrome, as well as even helping individuals with serious longstanding health conditions to arrive at a state of well-being.

THRIVING IN THE BALANCE OF LIFE AND DEATH: ONE WOMAN'S STORY OF COMFORT IN THE UNKNOWN

Two years ago, Debbie participated in a ten-session webinar on "The Healing Power of Mind" that I co-led with Ann Ross. This is her story:

> "I was deeply involved in my Christian mega church—I was writing and teaching small group bible study and was not really searching for anything when one of my dear friends suggested I check out the Three Principles. One day, as I listened to a Principles webinar, I was washed in a deep sense of peace. The more I listened, the more clarity I got and the more my faith got deeper. Over the next year, I learned to hear and respect my inner wisdom, those nudges of insight we get from time to time.

> "Later, I attended a Three Principles training with Rudi and Jules Kennard which unleashed a fountain of creativity within me. I decided to develop a curriculum on resilience for middle schools to help teens in these challenging times. Another 'nudge' inspired me to videotape all our team and student training sessions, in spite of initial resistance.

> "Fast forward a year; while recovering from knee surgery, I came down with sepsis, Babesia, Covid-19 and C. diff. Initially, I was immobilized by my illness and surgery, but I was grateful I had listened to divine

wisdom as I was able to keep creating training programs using the videos I had recorded in the past.

"Although I was in extreme pain and totally incapacitated, I felt a deep peace within. My joints were 'red hot,' and nothing would relieve my physical pain, but in the midst of the intense discomfort, I felt no suffering. I now receive 24-hour palliative care while medical experts are trying to figure out the diagnosis and treatment plan."

Debbie decided that given her uncertain prognosis, since she didn't know how long she would be alive, she was guided to release all of her work. Teams of people appeared to help her do what she could not do for herself; miracle after miracle happened.

Years ago, music had started to come to Debbie. She wrote the lyrics to ten songs and called the worship music director to ask if he was interested in going through them. Synchronistically, just that morning he had been praying for more new music before Debbie's phone call came. He loved her lyrics, and as he read them, melodies to go with her words came to him.

A few Sundays later, watching the church service on Zoom, Debbie saw members of the congregation singing her songs, many moved to tears. Debbie was overjoyed knowing that her music had touched them so deeply. The worship music leader told her that he would include her songs in his next album. His last gospel album had been ranked in iTunes Top 10.

That same day, Debbie's new book came out, titled, *And God Said… Wisdom, Hope, and Love from the Heart of God.* Her book records the divine answers that come to her while journaling during her time seeking God's wisdom. It was surprising how quickly the book came together.

It seemed that the more Debbie listened to the inner voice of wisdom and insight, the more things started to fall into place. For instance, one day, she felt the nudge to call an old friend who worked at BECON TV (the local public television channel working with regional schools and the community) and tell her about the teen mental health videos. After watching the videos, her friend decided to air them on the South Florida network. They will be shown to more than five million viewers between segments for a full year.

"It makes no sense; it takes no effort on my part. I have no energy and am in constant pain, yet now all this is happening almost by grace. In the midst of my body becoming weaker from illness, my spirit thrives stronger each day. I feel an aliveness and creativity that is almost unimaginable. I can feel sadness and joy at the same time. I can hold physical un-wellness simultaneously with spiritual wellness. My life is a kaleidoscope of experiences.

"After Halloween, I felt worse and worse and didn't think I could make it till Christmas. I asked my husband if he could decorate the house early for the holidays. He said, 'Why not?' And so in the beginning of November, we had our grandchildren over in their Christmas pajamas, which was great fun. They loved celebrating an early Christmas, and I needed to be surrounded by their joy and love. We had the best day.

"Now, after a lifetime of fearing death, I am not afraid. End of life is not a failure. I only sense a graduation to eternity. Whatever trials I've been given, I've also been given, by God's grace, the power to walk through them."

Debbie said she had contacted me because she felt called to do this interview for my book:

"Your teaching me about my innate resilience, that I will have the wisdom I need when I need it, has been revealed to me time and time again. Before, I walked deeply with the Holy Spirit and felt a deep presence knowing He would carry me through, but I didn't know about my resilience. Then I began to realize I was not my illness, my diagnosis, my emotions; that I didn't have to control the future and have things 'just so.' There is a part of me that is untouched by circumstances and symptoms, the part that is made in the image and likeness of God. I feel grief over the loss of six friends these past few months due to Covid and cancer, yet at the same time, I feel untouched by it. When I see who I really am, I settle down, because who I really am rises up within me. The Three Principles are what opened up a whole new level of experience to me in spite of my illness.

"Many problems I have faced while being ill have opened up a higher level of creativity within me because of my understanding of the Principles. The desire to help others through the teen curriculums, the faith-based Three Principles videos, the book and songs I wrote, and the opportunities I have had to be of service all came from the divine voice in my heart that said, 'Do this!' and from ignoring the voices of ego and habit that said, 'No, not me!' I trusted wisdom over the voices in my head from the past."

"One of the things I teach and have learned myself is to discern wisdom from the hurricane of personal thoughts in my head," Debbie related, and then went on to share one more poignant example from her own life to illustrate the discernment:

"I got this overwhelming feeling [I should] not go on the medication that the doctors thought was a good option. I asked God, the divine intelligence behind life, to show me in a way that I would understand what was troubling me. Then it occurred to me to look up the contraindications of this medication they were recommending. Sure enough, the things in my blood work that showed up positive were contraindicated for this drug."

When Debbie shared this with the doctor, her physician was shocked and said, "Oh my, you're right!" Wisdom had guided Debbie once again, perhaps even saving her life.

"I used to think I had to get quiet to hear my wisdom, now I see it differently. Even when your mind is full of chatter, wisdom can swoop in, and all the noise quiets down instantly. I can't look for wisdom in my personal thoughts, the hurricane of my mind, I just lean into God's love where wisdom resides. And it will come in the perfect time of the perfect way."

Debbie's story of living with pain and the possibility of her life ending is a powerful example of the inner strength of resilience in action. I have spoken with many people over the years who have had a similar experience as they face the ultimate fear of death. Each story has the common denominator of learning to recognize the thinking that is coming from fear of the unknown and letting that thought go. And then out of the blue comes this feeling of deep peace, a knowing that all is well, no matter the outcome.

When our mind is at peace, we suffer less. When our mind is hypervigilant, worried, and stressed, our body's immune system is compromised. Understanding the mind/body connection is a major factor in the healing process.

Ordinary Awakenings: We've all heard that our state of mind affects our bodies, and that mental stress lowers our immune system. But have we really listened deeply to what this means? Has it dawned on us that the weight of unnecessary negative thinking is pushing our immune system down like a backpack full of rocks, adding insult to our physical injuries? What if we set the pack down so our immune system could rise to the higher level of function for which it was designed?

Consider the possibility that thought and the body are actually connected, and see what happens the next time you are physically unwell.

CHAPTER 7

HEALING FROM THE PAST: TRAUMA, ADDICTION, AND ABUSE

"What happened in the past may have influenced our present-day personal or social problems, but please believe me, there is no answer to these problems in the past. Only in the now can the answer be found.

"The intensity and importance of such events dissipates as we see that the past is no longer a reality, but a memory carried through time via our own thoughts."

—Sydney Banks, *The Missing Link*

I spent the first decade of my career as a psychologist counseling people who had experienced many traumas, addictions, and experiences, believing that if they were made aware of what in the past had caused their present suffering, they would be free of it. I would encourage my clients to relive the past and go into great detail reliving painful memories in the hopes of healing the wounds of the past. It was a very painful process both for my clients and for me as a counselor.

There seemed to be no end to digging into their past to try to achieve a happy life in the present. Some would experience temporary relief, but when their symptoms came back, I would dig deeper for something that we had clearly missed so they could realize mental health. Therapy became a lifelong process for many of our clients. That seemed normal and a necessary evil for psychotherapists like me. "No pain, no gain" was the motto of the day.

When I listened to Syd Banks forty years ago, I realized that psychology had it backward. The solution was not to be found reliving and re-experiencing the past, but in each person seeing their thoughts in the moment as the creation of their psychological experience, not an effect of the past experience that they were thinking about. Awakening to seeing the true source of their experience liberated those whom I worked with from having to relive the past and allowed them to move into the present moment, where true mental health resides. The transformations in my clients shocked me as I saw the simplicity of Syd's Principles applied to helping those with serious histories and mental health diagnoses. My clients got well more quickly and with less painful therapy.

The following are a sampling of stories of people who have suffered greatly from abuse, trauma, addiction, and severe mental illness and how the Principles got them on the road to transformation.

MARCIA'S STORY OF REBIRTH FROM A LIFE OF TRAUMA

"I was a normal happy child until age six. That's when I was kidnapped and sexually abused for three years. After I was rescued, I built a big protective wall around myself to feel emotionally safe. I trusted nobody but myself. My whole life for the next forty years was a series of broken relationships, disappointments, crime, poverty, divorce, and many suicide attempts. I was constantly scanning my surroundings for my abductor and imagined most men as molesters. Most of my life, I was all mixed up and had to see psychiatrists and psychotherapists, but I wasn't getting better. I got no relief from my misery.

"As an adult, I searched and searched, trying to reconnect with that lovely person I had been before this all happened. After many failed relationships, I gave up. I just wallowed in my misery and got into trouble with the law.

"Luckily, through the legal system, I ended up in a course on the Three Principles for women offenders. And then, wow! What I heard not only changed my life, it saved my life. I would have either been dead or in prison for life if I hadn't changed. This course literally stopped me in my tracks. The simplicity of the Principles overwhelmed me. What was holding me back was not my past, but my thoughts!

"And then I thought, 'If it's that simple, why hasn't anyone told me this before? Oh my God, this is the most powerful thing I've ever seen in my life.' I've seen power in the world, people thinking they are strong, but this is way more powerful than that. It's like a force that you don't know is even there, and it took me, and I thought, 'Oh my God, I'm in.'

"I'm not the same person I was. I'm jolly, I'm happy; I want to live my life. I'm happy with my son now. I'm living the most amazing life. It's like winning the lottery. I'm poor and don't have a lot of money, but I'm doing so many things I've never done before. Now I am helping so many people just like me by sharing what I have learned. I think I can tackle anything that comes my way.

"People ask me, 'What's your secret? Why are you so happy?' And I say, 'It's kind of like the clouds in the sky. We know they're there, but we can't touch them. We can focus on one and see a shape appear, and then it will pass, and we'll see another, which will also float away. It's that way with your thoughts.'

"I am a new woman. This has given me a new life. I want other people to feel like I do. I don't want them to feel that they are broken, no matter how bad their past abuse or trauma. Their life can be whole again like mine. It's like snapping your fingers and your whole life changes. It's so simple. Basically, I've always been this way inside, and it was other things that blocked me, like those clouds getting in the way of the sun. Before I knew it, I was teaching others about the Three Principles, and it was taking over my life in a good way. I was beaming with a light radiating from within, and I felt like I'd been cleansed from the inside out."

Marcia's story, though miraculous, is not unusual. Her experience is happening in prisons and correctional facilities in many parts of the world. The simplicity and practicality of the Principles transcends age, ethnicity, religion, nationality, and diagnosis. However severe the conditions leading up to a person's messed-up life, with love and true understanding, any trauma, wound, or hurt can be healed and the person returned to their original state. This is the resiliency of the human spirit.

TOMMY'S STORY OF TRAUMA AND DRUG ADDICTION

This is the remarkable story of a man's journey to health after his discovery of the Three Principles.

> "When I was four, my mom and dad divorced. Two years later, on my first day of school, I was brutally beaten by two older students. After that, I hated going to school. My dad was an alcoholic, and my mom was always working, so I was raised by my sisters.

> "When I was age ten, my mom and sisters were all killed in a car accident. In one moment, my whole world was stripped away from me. My whole personality and character changed. I became very insecure and miserable.

> "When I graduated from high school, I saw my friends using drugs. They looked happy and I wanted what they had, and so it began, my life with drugs. I experimented with alcohol, marijuana, cocaine, and amphetamines. For the next eighteen years, I was an addict.

"I was arrested three times, and the third time was the one that woke me up. On that day, sitting in my car with one pocket full of drugs and the other full of money, I realized how miserable I was. I had nice cars and a house, but I was dead inside. These things didn't give me what I had been searching for all my life. I was open to something new, prison or not.

"The cop who arrested me said, 'Tom, you know you are looking at a felony and eight years in prison.' And I smiled. He thought I must be high because I looked so happy, but I just knew I was done with that life of drugs. It was over.

"When I was released, I was ordered to attend 108 Narcotics Anonymous meetings. After a while, I noticed that the group members were always focusing on what was wrong with themselves rather than what was positive inside. So I asked if there were other types of meetings I could go to. The counselor said yes and sent me to a Three Principles class called Health Realization. I didn't go too deep into the pool of what they were saying, but I heard enough to realize that what was going on in my life was all happening within my own head.

"After the course, I visited an old using friend's house trailer and saw a friend of his lying on the same couch where I used to do drugs. The guys sitting there asked me if I wanted to get high on meth. The old feelings of using popped into my head, and I could feel the rush of desire. But then the next thought was about the Three Principles. I remembered that this temptation was just a thought, and I knew I didn't want that anymore because I had found true happiness inside myself. I didn't need the drugs anymore to get that feeling.

"Then I had this huge insight. Why wasn't I using that moment with my friends? Because I was finally happy. I didn't need drugs to be happy. I was free of my addiction. That's why I said no.

"Since then, I have come to realize that the worst day I have now off drugs is far better than the best day I ever had on drugs."

Tommy's story of addiction started with a real and traumatic series of events. Drug addiction only numbed the negative feelings temporarily. His transformation reawakened his innate health, his true essence, and the source of his natural well-being and resilience.

WENDY'S JOURNEY OUT OF ADDICTION AND PROSTITUTION

"I lived a pretty normal and happy life as a young married woman with a small child. I was going to nursing school and working in the medical profession. However, in the early 1980s, I somehow started using drugs. I don't really remember a specific time or day. It just seems that somehow drugs came into my life and took over.

"I ended up on the streets, homeless, a crack-addicted prostitute with an extensive arrest record; I landed in jail around seventy-two times, four times in prison, and many, many times in institutions and drug treatment centers. My parents paid so much money for any kind of drug treatment they could find 'fix' me. Nothing helped. I changed religions. I changed locations. I bounced between NA and AA meetings. I tried all the latest metaphysical treatments. I changed diets. I was just floundering for over twenty-five years, trying to get well, all the time digging myself deeper and deeper into addiction, pain, and misery. The doctors labeled me with all sorts of mental health diagnoses.

"In 2003, I met some great people who introduced me to a wonderful man named Syd Banks. His philosophy seemed so simple and easy that it was too good to be true. However, I finally grasped the important fact that all the things I had been searching for to fix me weren't necessary because I really wasn't broken. I already had everything I needed inside me to drastically change my life from the inside out.

"I have been off drugs and living a beautiful, peaceful, and harmonious life since 2004. I never went back to drugs or to the dregs of my homeless hell on the streets. My whole world changed when I learned the Three Principles and started applying them to my life. Everything I had searched for, paid for, and got high to find was inside me the whole time. The Three Principles have changed my life. I am so grateful today."

Wendy's story of healing from her addiction demonstrates the power of our innate resilience to heal us, no matter how severe and serious our addiction or mental health issues. The old saying, "When the student is ready, the teacher appears" is applicable in all these stories. This readiness is the willingness and/or openness to hear and see something that will break the trance of our habits of thinking and doing. The understanding of how the Mind actually works to create our unique separate reality frees us from the prison of our personal thought system: our ego.

The next story, that of Bryan, illustrates the notion of readiness and the understanding that it's never too late to change. Bryan was introduced to the Principles through me and Sydney Banks at the young age of only fifteen years old, but it wasn't until he became mentally ill and addicted and ended up in a Three Principles treatment center that he woke up to his True Self.

BRYAN'S STORY: I AM NOT BROKEN

"I entered the Gulf Breeze Recovery program on July 6, 2014. At age forty-two, I was on six different psychiatric medications plus alcohol. I was spiritually, mentally, and physically sick, overweight, and on heavy doses of most of my medications. Dr. Amen's Clinic had diagnosed me one year earlier as ADD and Bipolar II with Generalized Anxiety Disorder. I had also self-disclosed as an alcoholic. Up to this point, I had spent a majority of my life being anxious, depressed, and addicted. I was selfish, heading for divorce, and suicidal. In the morning, while fixing my kids' food, I would hold a knife and think about killing myself.

"The first week I was in treatment, my wife said she wanted to send me divorce papers. At the time, I didn't even care, I was so numb. After sobering up in treatment, with the help of my counselor, I started to care again. I started to feel the pain of my actions. Even though my wife still planned on divorcing me, she was talking to me while I was in treatment. She even attended online meetings once a week.

"This was a very hard time for my family, especially for my two daughters. I had left home a month before treatment so I could drink full-time and engage in other addictive behaviors. While in treatment, I would talk to my daughters on a regular basis. My youngest one, Megan, just kept saying, 'Come home daddy' in the sweetest voice. I would go up into my room at night and pray and cry while looking at their pictures.

"I had left my wife in a mess with credit card debt and two kids to care for while she was working full-time. We had tried traditional marital and parenting counseling as well as twelve-step support groups. Nothing had seemed to work.

"Two weeks into treatment, I spoke to the staff about leaving early. I told them that I was needed at home and that I thought I could continue the program there on my own. They said it was good that I was feeling remorse, but that I really should complete the two-month program. I was told that once I found my own wisdom, life would fall into place and it would be safe to return home. For some reason, I believed them and decided to stay and commit to the program. Two more weeks passed, and I started to experience a bit of improvement in my mood. I started to see that being/living in the present moment was the full package. I requested for my wife to hold off the divorce for one month till after I got home so she could just spend time with me and see that I was truly different and had really changed this time. She agreed.

"On August 4, during the morning session, I was in a good mood and feeling present. The counselor put on a video of Panache Desai being interviewed by Oprah on Super Soul Sunday. The speaker spoke emotionally about God's unconditional love for us and that we are not broken. I felt like he was speaking directly to me, and I could feel the words. I instantly felt unconditional love wash over me and I started to weep. I knew at that moment that it was true. God loves me no matter what, and I am not broken. That same day, I called my wife after lunch and we talked about God for a half hour. I felt deep joy and love.

"The very next day, we talked by video call, and I spoke from my heart and soul. I said words I don't remember to this day. The feelings I had for her just poured out of me. That was the moment our marriage began to recover. I felt elated. I knew that regardless of what happened I would have a friend for life. It was a win/win situation. I told my counselor later that this had been the best day of my life. In fact, a year later in 2015, we renewed our marriage vows on that very day.

"The counselors ended up being right about suggesting that I stick out the treatment and not leave early. I continued to make good progress in my treatment. During this time, I reacquainted myself with Sydney Banks. I read *The Enlightened Gardener* and was deeply affected by the messages it held for me. I progressed more quickly and deeply and found my own positive feeling and my own wisdom. The doctors were able to dramatically reduce my medications. My treatment was coming to an end.

"On August 30, 2014, I left treatment knowing deep within that it was time to go home and join my wife up north for a camping trip. The kids were staying with friends. We hiked together and talked at dinner as friends, truly enjoying each other's company for the first time in years.

"It struck me how one year prior I'd had the exact same life circumstances, but now I was living life with a fresh new outlook. I felt joy and had a sense of humor again. I cried a lot and still do, but it's out of love and gratitude for my life. I smile more, and it feels good to be alive and awake. I started writing and posting messages and quotes on Facebook, and people have really responded positively to my messages. I started inspiring people with my story and inspirational and spiritual quotes.

"My daughter Norah told me she likes the 'new' daddy better. I didn't even tell her that I'd changed; she noticed it on her own. My wife loves the change in me although at times she has said it is unnerving. She had been with me since 1999, and now I was suddenly a new person.

"Every aspect of my life has improved: my financial situation, my mood, my weight, my overall health, my level of satisfaction with life, my relationships, and my work. I still have low moods, but they aren't as bad and don't last as long. I feel my negative emotions now and just let them pass through.

"I give back by sharing my story with Gulf Breeze guests on a regular basis. I am part of a Three Principles group in Denver, Colorado, that I am the chair of currently. I enjoy writing and have found that touching the lives of others by inspiring them or giving them little reminders can be a precious gift. I never knew I could write until October of 2014.

"I truly believe there is a feeling that guides us from the cradle to the grave and we just need to listen to its guidance. I often feel like a soul surfer riding waves of gratitude, love, joy, and compassion. I know this is only the beginning."

Bryan recently shared his story at an international conference on the Three Principles and addiction. He has written a book of spiritual and inspirational quotes called *Matters of the Soul*, available on Amazon. Having known Bryan since he was a teenager, I have witnessed his story of transformation unfold over a lifetime. His parents have gone on this journey with him, and they now lead a loving support group in Minnesota based on the Three Principles for people with addictions and their loved ones.

The road to recovery and true serenity is never exactly the same, but with an understanding of the Principles and the process of transformation, we have a compass and a map to get us back on track. We are never really lost, we only think we are.

We are only one thought, one insight away from true freedom and the ability to thrive in the uncertainty of our daily lives. Many of my clients who suffer from addiction and other traumas see these Principles as a "gift" of understanding that can truly heal their lives.

These three examples are true, and their stories can be your story too. We are all capable of transformation at any moment. It is not a matter of willpower or luck, but of "insight," a *sight from within* showing us the true nature of our human experience. Insight is not under our control but comes from a state of willingness and openness coupled with a true understanding of the nature of human experience. This insight can be the trigger that awakens our potential for change and transformation. Everyone can thrive, no matter their past trauma or limited opportunities.

Ordinary Awakenings: There's always reason for hope. Considering that transformation is possible for anyone, regardless of situation or length of time, is there a challenge in your life for which you would like to see new possibilities reawakening your own innate resilience?

CHAPTER 8

TRANSFORMING OUR WORLD WITH WISDOM

*"Mankind cannot solve its problems at the
level of thinking that created the problem."*

This chapter will address how a shift in our understanding of Mind
not only facilitates our own transformation from personal struggle
to resilience, but it can facilitate changes in those with whom we are
in contact, both in our workplaces and communities. I will share
stories of resilience in action from within prison systems and other
high-risk populations.

This quoted sentiment by Gandhi sums up the message of this
chapter: "If we could change ourselves, the tendencies in the world
would also change. As a man changes his own nature, so does the
attitude of the world change towards him." When I first heard of
the Principles in 1980, they impacted me on a personal level. As
a therapist and psychology trainer, I immediately saw the power
of this understanding to help those I was serving. I knew I had
changed but had no idea how to pass on this profound realization
to others. I felt hope and enthusiasm and was excited to learn how
to teach this new understanding. To accomplish this, I signed up for
a year-long internship in Miami, Florida, at the Advanced Human

Studies Institute. I had hundreds of questions about how to teach the Principles and how this could apply to my work with clients with addictions, mental health challenges, and abuse issues.

My teachers responded to each eager question with a simple, "Joe, you have to catch the ball before you run with it." I knew this was true, but in my mind, I was always trying to figure out how to apply it to my clients. I thought my approach was both practical and selfless. They persisted patiently, nudging me to quiet down and really hear this for myself. "Be the change you want to see in others." It was a hard pill for me to swallow, with my lifelong pattern of wanting to help and fix others. I felt the weight of trying to shift my entire way of counseling toward this new paradigm.

As time went on, insight by insight, I began to "catch the ball" and realize my own mental health and resilience on a deeper level. As I did, I shared with my clients from my own newfound understanding. The results were remarkable; I didn't feel like I was doing much of anything, but what I was saying from my own depth of understanding was impacting them in ways I had never experienced before. The simplicity of the Principles helped my clients find their own mental health. That had always been my goal in the first place, but I never dreamed the process could be so effortless and quick. Soon my practice grew to the point where I had to start a mental health center and hire and train a large staff. I was having an impact beyond anything I had ever imagined from my years of psychological training.

My story is not unique. Over the past forty years I have had the privilege of teaching this understanding to a wide variety of change agents—addiction counselors, social workers, therapists, medical professionals, police, firefighters, business leaders, educators, and many more. It is my hope that through these stories, you will gain hope, vision, and inspiration to find your own resilience and the vision to pass it on to others.

ONE WOMAN'S TRANSFORMATION BRINGS THE PRINCIPLES TO PRISONERS AND OTHER DISADVANTAGED COMMUNITIES AGAINST ALL ODDS

Beverley Wilson Hayes's personal transformation lifted her out of a twelve-year relationship with drugs, showing unmistakably that innate health and guidance lies within us all regardless of our circumstances. Even before Beverley discovered the Three Principles, she knew she had to walk away from a lifestyle of addiction. The depth of her transformation led her to a life of leadership in her community. She wanted to help others like herself and began to contribute time to starting groups, programs, and halfway houses for women and children.

An early insight in her recovery moved her forward. "I know there has to be more than the Twelve Steps to facilitate recovery," she often thought. Eventually, this was confirmed when she discovered and was trained in the Three Principles. At the time, as the only African American person trained in this model in the state of California, she contributed greatly to the advancement of the Principles. Beverley continued to achieve other professional goals, such as completing her master's degree in Community Economic Development.

Dr. Mark Howard and I were conducting a training program for the Santa Clara County Drug and Alcohol Division of Human Services on the Three Principles and addiction after the release of my book

The Serenity Principle. I'd heard of Beverley's renowned work in revitalizing one of the most dangerous high-risk communities in the Oakland, California, area and invited her as a guest speaker. Beverley's profound transformation and her experiences mesmerized the conference participants. We have been dear friends ever since. Here is the story she shared with me:

"MIRACLE ON 66TH AVENUE"—A STORY OF THE TRANSFORMATION OF A HOUSING PROJECT CALLED COLISEUM GARDENS

Coliseum Gardens was a housing project near the Oakland Coliseum in Oakland, California, a neighborhood considered by the police to be a war zone. The drug dealers would throw rocks and bottles from the rooftops onto police cars entering the gates of the project. These criminals ran the housing project, which provided housing mostly to African American and Cambodian refugee residents. The streetlights were all broken, the grass was long gone from lack of upkeep, exposing the bare ground, and graffiti was everywhere. It was bleak and filled with poverty, crime, and feelings of hopelessness. At least two dead bodies were found weekly near the dumpsters. After the mayor of Oakland read about the Modello Project in Homestead Gardens, Florida, he asked the East Bay Community Recovery Project to replicate the same program in Coliseum Gardens. Taking into account Beverley's prior successes, she was chosen to head the program. Dr. Roger Mills was also hired to conduct resident and staff training.

The Modello project in Dade County, South Florida, was similar in nature to Coliseum Gardens. It had been transformed into a healthy community through the work of Dr. Roger Mills, who had brought the Three Principles to the residents of this high-risk, high crime community. Janet Reno, Bill Clinton's Attorney General, became curious about this program after it was covered by Bryant Gumbel in a *Today Show* special. She later visited Beverley's program in California.

I was able to meet the residents of this community while I was an intern in Coral Gables. It stood out like the "Emerald City" next to the neighboring housing projects' desolation, which Modello had previously mirrored. After the residents began to see how the Principles work in everyday life, they transformed their homes, their schools, and their lives. (A book was written about Modello called *Modello: A Story of Hope for the Inner City and Beyond* by Dr. Jack Pransky. In 2001, this book won the Martin Luther King Storyteller's Award for the best book exemplifying Dr. King's vision of "the beloved community.")

Many other well-intentioned community workers had previously tried to help Coliseum Gardens, but they'd become discouraged at the immensity of the problems and give up after a couple of months. When Beverley first arrived at Coliseum Gardens, it took a while to gain residents' trust because they had previously experienced disappointments and dashed hopes. Their state of mind was depressed, fearful, and hopeless. Beverley saw this and insisted that the city would stick with her project long-term to build trust.

Beverley started with focus groups called, "Girls, let's talk." With these groups, she built rapport and trust with the matriarchs of the community and other residents. Eventually they started what they called "Health Realization classes" on the Three Principles. Beverley's work was grounded in her own innate resilience, giving her a "bullet proof" power to face extensive resistance. She saw the resilience of those she was teaching, and eventually they began to see and experience it in themselves.

Beverley helped them see that all human beings are creating their own separate realities. This introduced her students to a very practical understanding based on the Principles of how thought works. Eventually, residents began to see that their thoughts, *not* their circumstances, were creating their moment-to-moment reactions, emotions, and behavior.

For example, the African American residents never spoke to the Cambodian residents. They believed that the government was giving the Cambodians special treatment, as they noticed the Cambodians were buying vans. Few of the Cambodians spoke English, which was another barrier. One day, Beverley met Chi, their leader and translator, and listened to his story. Chi had been tormented and tortured by the Khmer Rouge in Cambodia. He recounted tales of atrocities, starvation, and mass extinction at the hands of the regime, describing how he and a handful of others had managed to escape. His story so touched Beverley that she invited him and twenty-five other Cambodians to share these experiences with the Black and Latino residents who were attending the Health Realization classes.

The Black and Hispanic residents were deeply touched by these stories. The barriers between the ethnic groups began to crumble, and the racial divide eventually healed. In later sessions, Chi shared how the Cambodian residents had saved money by pooling their resources and eventually had enough to buy a van to share. They bought food in bulk which was equally divided among the families. He described how they had given up meat to save enough money to buy the first van and eventually several others for easy transport. The Black, Hispanic, and Cambodian residents began to greet each other and form friendships. All three groups mutually benefitted from each other's experiences and ideas.

Meanwhile, a community police officer, Jerry Williams, was assigned to work with the residents of Coliseum Gardens. Although he was trained in community policing, he had no idea how to implement his field of study in a practical sense until he met Beverley. When he witnessed the changes in the community, he became curious and started attending the Health Realization classes himself. Eventually, his whole team of officers joined him.

Jerry recognized some of the people he had previously arrested and recalled their hostility in the past; but now, they were friendly and courteous. Some residents in the class asked him, "What's your story?" He shared with them the reasons for the professional protocols governing his conduct when called in for a crime or domestic dispute. He explained why he did what he did to keep himself and them safe and unharmed. Once they heard his "separate reality" as a police officer, they understood why police did the things they did, and as a result, a trusting relationship was established. (See Jerry's story in the following section.)

As I said above, drug dealers controlled the community. Once the residents realized how much trouble those individuals brought, the residents put "wanted posters" around the neighborhood bearing the message: "Wanted—[the drug dealer's name and photo]—to leave the community." The posters were signed by the community members. Soon the unwanted dealers had all left for a more receptive drug dealing turf elsewhere.

Health was beginning to come to Coliseum Gardens in the form of cooperation and friendliness. Hope was in the air. Residents had a new attitude toward social services, and the social workers were much more responsive to their needs, such as making access to medical assistance and food stamp programs easier. The cold relationship that had existed for generations began to melt. Police were seen as helpers rather than the enemy. Jerry became known as "the Lollipop Cop," always handing out candy to the kids.

Coliseum Gardens as a whole was dismal looking, so Beverley decided to set up a focus group to get kids' input on what they envisioned their community could look like. They drew pictures of what it looked like now and how they wanted it to look. The first drawings were of broken streetlights, destroyed playground equipment, and big patches of bare ground. The second drawings contained their hopes for bright streetlights so the kids could play in the dark, green grass, flowers, fruit trees, toys, and playground equipment. When Beverley saw the children's drawings, her eyes welled up. The kids filled her with renewed hope and determination.

Soon, Beverley enlisted the broader community to donate plants, seeds, and playground equipment. Once the mental health of the community was restored, the outer reality began to change, exactly as it had in Modello. The mayor noticed the transformation, and he wasn't the only one. The *East Bay Express* did an exposé on the program called "Miracle on 66th Avenue," which caught the attention of others around California. Governor Jerry Brown invited Beverley Wilson Hayes and Jerry Williams to be guests at a special ceremony in Los Angeles where he presented Jerry with the California Peace Award. US Attorney General Janet Reno visited the project, and subsequently, President Bill Clinton invited Jerry to the White House in recognition of the project's success. Jerry always gave credit for the transformation to Beverley and the residents of Coliseum Gardens.

Since Modello and Coliseum Gardens, Beverley and many others have created similar projects—the Bronx, New York; Des Moines, Iowa; Minneapolis, Minnesota; Chicago, Illinois; Mississippi, South Carolina, and many more places. The real credit goes to the power of the Principles, which when once understood, can release the latent resilience in all human beings.

A COMMUNITY POLICE OFFICER DISCOVERS THE POWER OF THE PRINCIPLES IN TRANSFORMING HIS WORK: THE POWER OF CARING[1]

"Oakland Housing Authority police corporal Malcolm 'Jerry' Williams remembers when it was downright hazardous to patrol the Lockwood and Coliseum Gardens housing projects. Police routinely dodged bullets, rocks, and bottles and loathed having to drive through the complexes off 66th Avenue, even during the day. Residents, meanwhile, lived in fear amid drug deals and a murder rate that was the highest per capita in Oakland and fourth nationally.

"That was five years ago. Since then, no one has been slain in the two projects. The open-air drug markets are no more. And nowadays Williams, 50, is met with waves and smiles from a grateful citizenry because he helped turn everything around. The formula was simple: Williams set up a community policing office at Lockwood Gardens and started listening to residents. Together, they thought up novel ways to reduce crime and change the community for the better.

---

1   Story edited from *East Bay Express* newspaper article.

"For his pivotal role in the community's revival, Williams received a $25,000 California Peace Prize from the California Wellness Foundation. The award, which honors those who work to prevent violence in their communities, is a recognition that's well-deserved, residents say.

" 'Jerry is one-of-a-kind,' said Bernestine Robinson, 43. 'He listens to your problems—just because he has a badge and suit on, he doesn't let that be the reason.' Dale Burrell, 34, was a cocaine addict and in danger of getting evicted. Then he got some counseling from Williams. 'He bailed me out on a lot of things—I owe him my life,' said Burrell, adding he hasn't used drugs for three years.

"A burly, barrel-chested officer, Williams has an engaging banter and a quick, easy smile. On a walk through Lockwood Gardens recently, he was greeted with shouts of 'Hi Jerry,' hugged babies, and got some good-natured ribbing for the money he won. It was a decidedly different setting when Williams first came to the projects as an undercover narcotics officer buying drugs from dealers. 'This place used to be like Beirut,' Williams said. 'The people in this community were being held hostage in their own home.'

"Williams earned a degree in administration of justice from California State University at Hayward. After a stint in counseling, he joined the force in 1986 and quickly gained a reputation as a tough, no-nonsense cop. His drive and arrest rate got him promoted to corporal. He was then assigned to work as a community policing officer, a job description foreign to him at the time.

"As he cruised his beat in the projects, Williams was met with open hostility. He knew something had to be done, but thought it was a daunting task because no one seemed to respect the police. Then Williams attended a meeting taught by Beverley Wilson Hayes, a former resident of the projects. The session introduced him to the concept of 'Health Realization,' in which one's inner potential is used to solve problems. 'You look at the good in people, the innate mental health that is a birthright,' Williams said. 'Once they realize they have it, they can tap into it.' Williams acknowledges that the *Health Realization* program, pioneered by Dr. Roger Mills of Saratoga, is a far cry from the traditional concepts taught to new officers.

" 'Most police officers have a military style of training, and when you're trained like that, everybody becomes an enemy, as in the concepts of the *War on Drugs* and *War on Violence*,' he said. Williams, an eleven-year veteran of the Housing Authority police, said he changed himself—and the community noticed. Before, he was simply a conditioned police officer, just another cop in a car racing from one call to another. These days, Williams is known as 'Officer Friendly,' a caring cop who keeps candy in the trunk of his car. It was easier for him to change than to try to change the community.

"His rapport with the community has produced tangible results. In 1993, Williams and residents put up 'wanted' posters with the pictures of four drug dealers who controlled the neighborhood. The dealers, unaccustomed to the spotlight, soon left the area and never came back. There hasn't been a drug-related murder since then in the projects where there were four killings as recently as 1991.

"Williams has trained more than 1,000 police officers under the Health Realization program, encouraging them not to focus on the bad side of people but rather to accentuate the good side. His efforts have been recognized by President Clinton, who shook his hand during a visit to Washington. Attorney General Janet Reno has visited the projects twice. The City of Oakland was awarded 25 million dollars due to the success of their programs. Oakland's Lockwood and Coliseum Gardens were fourth in the nation in homicide and violent crimes prior to this transformation.

"For Williams, it was his personal transformation in policing philosophy that made it all possible. 'To establish partnerships with the community, I had to change—it was easier than changing the community,' he said. They thought, 'Here's a person who cares.' That's what turned everything around."

FINDING FREEDOM ON THE INSIDE (OF PRISON)

Beverley and her colleague Cathy Casey were invited by Robert Garner, head of the Department of Drug and Alcohol Division of Santa Clara County in California, to work with a group of Level 4 inmates at the county corrections facility. These prisoners, the most difficult in the facility, were often called "three-time losers" because of their multiple arrests and recidivism. As a big, angry, hostile audience, they were intimidating, but not to Beverley and Cathy; they had a powerful secret. They knew that each human being is born whole, resilient, perfect, and always has access to their innate health. Even though any person can lose sight of or cover up their beautiful inner selves, that essence can never be destroyed. Beverley and Cathy felt confident, courageous, and filled with hope and love for the inmates.

At first it was slow going, but they continued to come back week after week, never losing hope. Some of the inmates were catching on to what they were saying, even before these men saw it in themselves. You could tell because their facial expressions began to shift. Their eyes and faces seemed to emanate light, and the initial resistance they had put up changed to an attitude of curiousness and openness. Three of the inmates were chosen to be facilitators to help their fellow inmates because of their progress toward transformation. One inmate shared how his attitude toward his wife and the guards had changed through his newfound insight.

> "I realized that all my visits with my wife went badly, as well as why she always stormed out after a brief visit. I noticed I was always thinking negative thoughts about her and the kids and would criticize her as soon as she walked in the door. Until I took these classes, I never even knew that I was thinking, and it was my thinking that was making me so negative. I started to back off from those thoughts and saw her differently and began to give her compliments. Our visits lasted much longer and were very satisfying. I began to have 'sunlight thoughts;' out of the blue, I saw things with more wisdom."

This same inmate also started to see the human being behind the guard's uniform. That leveled the playing field. "I never saw them as human beings, just the enemy. Through the classes, I realized that we are all the same inside; we are all operating from the same human principles."

The guards started to notice the changes in the inmates who attended the classes. They remembered when previous speakers had come to help the inmates and how these speakers had often begun to take on the prisoners' attitudes and become hopeless and negative about the situation.

"You two always come in here so happy and cheerful. We thought you must be on drugs and wondered what you were giving the inmates!" Soon the guards wanted their own classes to learn what the inmates were learning. The relationships between the prisoners and guards shifted over time to a positive, more respectful feeling.

Beverley shared how the Three Principles are like a *time-release capsule*. Inmates would change without trying to change. Just listening while attending the classes and reading some of the books provided created a deep desire to learn more. The inmates began talking amongst themselves about what they were learning; instead of playing spades or dominos, now their downtime began to be filled with discussions of how they were changing. One inmate said his letters to his family became like music filled with wisdom and positive feelings toward them. The families were impacted as well, and their relationships improved.

Later, Beverley and Cathy moved to a lower security prison with both men and women inmates. One woman they encountered had grown up in a very poor, abusive family. She and her many siblings had been told that they were "lower than dirt," and each was called a derogatory animal name. Hers was "dog." Although she was very beautiful on the outside, she felt ugly on the inside. After the fourth week in class, she emerged from the cocoon of her low self-esteem and began to radiate pure beauty.

One day, she stood up in class and shouted, "You mean to tell me that all that goodness and beauty I was born with is still there inside me?" Hope had pulled her out of her habitual thinking, and her innate health and resilience began to shine. She forgave her abusive mom, once she realized that her mom had acted from the same thought-based reality as she had. Her resilience popped to the surface; she stopped listening to the old self-deprecating voices and realized her inner potential. Now she teaches the Principles to women like herself who have lived lives of drugs and crime, their innate resilience smothered by negative thinking. She helps them discover the beauty and power that she found for herself.

These stories, even if they are not part of our own life history, demonstrate the universal innate human potential of resilience. Principles are constants, universal and predictable. The Principles are now being taught in other high-risk environments such as the Gaza Strip of Palestine, as well as by the Rebels for Peace Project, which works with gangs in Chicago, and EMIS in Israel, all sponsored by *OneSolution.Org* (noted in the resources section).

Ordinary Awakenings: Through these incredible stories of people from all walks of life around the globe, we see the common thread of our basic humanity. The stories illustrate what the Principles look like in action and how our unique human experience is created. Imagine yourself as a community member living in Coliseum Gardens or a prisoner in the Santa Clara jail. Imagine the hope you would feel listening to Beverley, Jerry, and Cathy, how their words would lift you out of despair to see the limitless possibilities ahead. Consider and reflect upon the fact that although our life circumstances appear different, the Principles remain constant.

CHAPTER 9

THE BURNOUT SOLUTION: RESTORING OUR RESILIENCE IN TRYING TIMES FOR HEALTHCARE PROFESSIONALS

"Physician, Heal Thyself."

—Jewish motto quoted by Jesus, Luke 4:23

The problem of burnout is complex and has huge implications for the future of healthcare in general. Burnout also affects helping professions other than medical personnel, specifically counselors, addiction specialists, first responders, and social workers. The current Covid-19 pandemic has created a greater sense of urgency in these challenging times for our frontline workers. The prolonged stress of a growing epidemic impacts our hospitals, nursing homes, schools, businesses, air travel, vacations, sports, the economy, the stock market, and our diminishing 401K accounts, as well as causing record unemployment. This in turn fuels an already growing epidemic of stress, fear, and burnout in our professional lives, our relationships, and society as a whole.

I have worked with many healthcare institutions such as the Mayo Clinic, North Memorial Hospital, East Lansing Hospital Systems, and at the University of Minnesota School of Medicine in their

"Inner Life of Healers" program under the auspices of the Center for Spirituality and Healing. In addition, I have done extensive professional development training in social service agencies, addiction treatment centers, and mental health institutions. I have witnessed the power of the Three Principles understanding being taught to a broad variety of professionals and have seen the powerful effect it has had on healing burnout and preventing stress for those who care for the sick, the addicted, the abused, the mentally ill, and victims of poverty.

In this chapter, I will focus on some stories and research on how understanding the Three Principles can effectively restore innate resilience in healthcare professions.

THE EPIDEMIC OF BURNOUT IN THE HELPING PROFESSIONS

Since I began my professional career as a psychologist in the 1970s, I have witnessed burnout statistics continuing to rise. Current estimates show that between 54 and 65 percent of physicians, nurses, and other allied healthcare professionals experience serious symptoms of burnout and stress. In a recent study, rates of physician burnout rose from 45 to 54 percent in three years (Tait Shantafelt, MD, Mayo Clinic Proceedings, 2015). Seventy percent of physicians would not recommend that a young person go into medicine.

Studies on other healthcare professionals such as psychologists, social workers, and addiction counselors reveal similar results. The rate of burnout for mental health workers is nearly 67 percent in the US and 54 percent in the United Kingdom. Addiction counselors last an average of five years and then report burnout rates of 65 percent, according to some studies. Studies of nurses in five countries consistently showed burnout rates of 40 percent. The problem of burnout in people-centered professions is not just a US phenomenon. According to the 2016 Bureau of Labor Statistics, it is an international problem. Although we don't have up-to-date statistics for this pandemic era, it is obvious that these numbers will be dwarfed by the current unprecedented pressures on our healthcare industry.

These statistics point to a burnout epidemic in our healing professions that leads to increased medical errors, malpractice suits, low morale, high turnover, lowered patient satisfaction, and mental health and addiction problems among caregivers. Medical error is contributing to a rising death rate in the United States. These problems contribute to the ever-increasing costs of healthcare, which puts a burden on our economy and negatively affects the quality of our lives.

Most recently, in the era of the Covid-19 pandemic, burnout significantly affects all of our human service and medical professions. Healthcare providers, nursing home employees, and prison workers have all been tested to the limits of their resilience. The inevitable levels of pandemic burnout will rise, unless helping professionals discover their inner resilience and how the mind creates our moment-to-moment experiences. Here is one example of how the Principles helped lower stress and burnout in a major healthcare institution.

THE ARIZONA RESILIENCE PROGRAM IN THE MAYO CLINIC OF ARIZONA

Several years ago, I created pilot programs with Dr. Keith Blevens for the Mayo Clinic in Arizona to address the issue of burnout called "The Resilient Physician Program" and "The Arizona Resiliency Program." Current research on the effectiveness of these programs is very promising. Survey results of past participants report that 64 percent ruminate less about challenges in their work, 75 percent report they rebound more quickly from adversity, 78 percent said the course was helpful in reducing stress and burnout, and 79 percent are less emotionally reactive to other people and circumstances. In addition, 92 percent said they would recommend this course to others. They report improved effectiveness, efficiency, and perspective, which facilitate better relationships with coworkers. They also find more ease in difficult conversations, better decision-making, which leads to better teamwork, and improved work/life balance. Here is a sample of some of the positive feedback from participants.

BURNOUT/STRESS

"I feel much calmer in general, and my life is more in balance. I am sleeping better and feeling better rested. This program gets at the root of stress and burnout, unlike other tools and techniques that just help you cope with existing stress. By understanding and recognizing the root of stress, my internal thinking in the moment, I am able to nip it in the bud. Other techniques aren't very helpful. They only add more things for me to do in my already busy life. Now I have a way to understand what stress and burnout actually are."

—Teresa C., DNP, RN Chief Nursing Officer, Mayo Clinic

LEADERSHIP

"I am now a calming influence on my employees and coworkers. I am less reactive emotionally when others lose their bearings, and I take things less personally, enabling me to be the calm/wise presence in the room. When I am calm, they calm down as well. This leads to clearer thinking under pressure, better teamwork and cooperation, and increased creativity and productivity. Before I took this course, I couldn't sleep at night and felt I wouldn't last another three months in my job as department head. Now that I understand the real cause of my stress, I know I can complete the rest of my tenure easily. And I sleep through the night."

—Terry T., MD, Chair, Anesthesiology Department, Mayo Clinic

DECISION-MAKING

"Decision-making is still challenging at times, but my thinking is much clearer. I feel more resolved about my decisions and deliver them with more confidence and ease. As a result, I get less blowback and resistance. Sometimes I feel like I am juggling ten balls in the air at once. What I learned about resilience helps me focus on one ball at a time. I feel more in control because I am not overwhelmed by thinking about all ten balls at once. 'One ball at a time' makes for more clarity and efficiency, and ultimately, I experience less stress and have more enjoyment in my job."

—Hugo V., MD, Chair, Hepatology Department, Mayo Clinic

RELATIONSHIPS

"I am a better listener and carry less ego into my interactions. I am more honest and frank while remaining sensitive. In difficult relationship interactions, I am now seeing where my reactions are coming from: the inside of my own thinking, rather than from others or outside circumstances. I have less compulsion to 'fix' others, but instead set better boundaries and am able to delegate vs. control everything and everyone."

—Dawn P., Director of Leadership Development, Mayo Clinic

PRESENCE

> "I have less distracted thinking, less regret, guilt, worry, and ruminating about 'what if' and 'if only.' I feel I have more focus and can give more attention to what is happening in the moment."
>
> —Molly K., MD, Family Physician, Mayo Clinic

CRUCIAL CONVERSATIONS

> "The Principles I learned at the seminar come to me at tough times and in crucial conversations. I know when I react emotionally to just pause and reflect, and then I can naturally see the situation from a calmer and wiser perspective."
>
> —Jan S., MD, Researcher, Chair, Aerospace Medicine Program, Mayo Clinic

LOCUS OF CONTROL

> "I feel back in control, and stress no longer has power over me. Circumstances, other people, and workload can no longer control my inner feelings. I now see that my thinking in the moment is always the cause of stress, no matter what is happening on the outside. My unnecessary thinking is falling away."
>
> —Lucas, MD, hepatologist

DEALING WITH DIFFICULT PATIENTS

Dr. Lucas shared a story with me about how changing his perception of a difficult parent of one of his patients made all the difference:

> "I had a patient who had seen many other liver specialists, and none had been able to help this young man. I was his last resort to get a liver transplant, or he would die. Moreover, I had been forewarned about his 'overbearing' mother who regularly came to the intake interviews with him. The records were filled with stories about her questionable behavior.
>
> "As expected, this young man's mother did come across as overbearing in our first interview. She constantly answered for my patient and interrupted the patient and me when I directly questioned him. I felt annoyed by her apparent lack of respect toward her son.
>
> "Just as I was going to ask her to leave the interview, I realized that these upsetting feelings had to be coming from my own thinking, not from her. Then it occurred to me that if I were in her place, I would perhaps be feeling and acting protective in the same way. I could see she was worried about her son and wanted the best for him. My heart went out to her, and without any effort, my feelings shifted from annoyance to compassion. My perception of her had shifted instantly, and I saw her as my ally, not my enemy.
>
> "Simultaneously, her behavior shifted as well. The more I listened to her with kindness, the more helpful and

cooperative she became. Seeing 'her reality,' rather than judging it, freed me from negative reactivity and I completed a successful assessment of my patient, with her help."

LOUISE'S STORY: A NURSE'S TRANSFORMATION FROM BURNOUT TO HELPING OTHERS FIND THE EYE OF THE HURRICANE

"The year 2020 with its Covid-19 pandemic has been one of the most challenging years in recent medical history. I have been an NHS nurse and senior healthcare manager in the UK for over twenty-five years and currently work in Northern Ireland. I am married and have four children. My husband is a frontline nurse.

"In 2010, fifteen years into my career, I 'hit the wall' with burnout. I was a super-responsible, type A, workaholic, controlling person and had become depressed and exhausted. I had to take three months out of work at the time and returned back to work to find that in less than two years, I was almost back where I started. I didn't take time off work at this stage, and to cope with my stress and burnout, I was prescribed antidepressant and anxiety medications since things had got to the stage of me needing to take benzodiazepines on a daily basis to attend work as my anxiety and stress were causing me a lot of distress.

"At this stage, I read every night before I went to bed to ward off insomnia, devouring all the self-help books for coping techniques I could find. Then I read a book about the Three Principles, and something within it really spoke to me. I decided to join a three-month course on the Principles given by a coach, Jamie Smart. During the first weekend training, I had my first major insight. Jamie spoke of two states of mind: 'LaLa Land' (meaning the future and the past), and the Present Moment. He said that the present moment is the only real time there is, the rest is an illusion of thought.

"I don't know what hit me, but I had a massive insight and felt a flood of emotions ranging from anger to relief. I asked myself, 'Why didn't I see this before? It's so obvious!' I cried for three hours grieving precious time lost in my 'LaLa Land' thinking. I became immersed in the Three Principles videos and books, absorbing all I could. Within six weeks, I was off all my depression and anxiety meds and knew I would never need them again. I had found true peace and contentment which would never go away even in times of momentary stress or getting caught up in 'LaLa Land.' Feeling resilient felt so natural, like I had come home.

"My coworkers and friends didn't have the same insight, and I noticed them innocently getting caught up in their thinking, as I had done my whole life. I felt empathy for them and wanted to help. In the past, I would have commiserated with them, taking on their stress and negativity and catching their mental flu. But instead, it was like I had been given a mental health vaccine to protect myself from the 'mental flu virus'! Now if I start going there, I catch myself and go back to my default setting of calm and resilience.

"The Principles have affected my whole life. As a parent, I was seen as the 'officer in charge,' barking orders and filling the house with wall-to-wall to-do lists. After all, my husband and I were both nurses and had four kids and an ailing mother to care for. Now I have shifted to a more lighthearted, happy, fun-loving and relaxed frame of mind. My husband and I are more connected than ever. I now see that my kids have the same wisdom as I do, so I don't worry so much about them. They are now reminding me when I get caught up in my thinking.

"I taught a class on the Principles at my twins' elementary school and used a metaphor of traffic lights to explain how our feelings and thinking are connected. 'Red' is telling you to stop, to not act on your insecure thinking. 'Yellow' is the warning light to make you aware to be cautious and realize where your feelings are coming from: your thinking. 'Green' tells you to trust your thinking and insight and wisdom and to go ahead. My twins are always reminding me, 'What color is your light, mom?' What I taught them is coming back to bite me. After all, we all innocently get caught in our emotions and thinking and need reminding from time to time.

"I have now become the lead for my National Health Service (NHS) healthcare organization in Northern Ireland in Quality Improvement. Last March, when the Covid-19 pandemic was realized, my colleagues and I headed up an initiative to support our frontline medical staff, and I found that my ongoing conversations were steeped in the Principles' understanding of how life works. We developed a resource for our physicians called 'Doctors Hub,' a point of contact for physicians to help them deal with stress and burnout in a preventative way before it occurs. This resource offers doctors support in whatever way helps them stay focused and unstressed in their high demand jobs. During the pandemic, we would help them get tested for Covid-19 if need be, or find housing if they needed to be quarantined from their families for a time.

"We are also implementing group sessions on psychological well-being and interviewing people throughout the system at all levels of the organization who have found ways to deal with the pressure in a healthy way. In addition, I am also implementing weekly podcasts with experts from outside and within our NHS system to talk about burnout prevention and share other useful information by creating a space to allow for insight for our healthcare staff.

"I realized that I can't just come in and shove the Principles down people's throats. I have to meet them where they are, have a conversation, and listen. When they become curious, I can gently point them in the direction of realizing where their psychological experiences are coming from."

Louise made me smile as she continued in that Irish way of hers. "A puppy is not just for Christmas. And mental well-being is not just for the time of Covid-19. Resilience is something that's already there in all of us. It's not like a tiny seedling you have to water and fertilize. The plant inside each of us is already in full bloom and unbreakable. It will always carry us through whatever life brings. We simply have to calm down and realize through a quiet mind that all the answers lie within already. Our insight is always available. There are unlimited possibilities."

THE VACCINE TO PREVENT STRESS AND BURNOUT: A NURSE'S TRANSFORMATION

Teresa is a post-anesthesia recovery nurse in a rural part of Texas. Before she attended Dr. Keith Blevens's seminar on the nature of resilience and the Principles that govern it, she was suffering from debilitating chronic pain, severe work stress, and multiple family crises—a daughter with alcoholism, a husband with war-related PTSD, and another daughter going through a divorce. She was driven by worry and the need to give advice in order to "fix" them all.

Teresa coped with her stress and pain through numerous holistic practices such as massage, bodywork, and the use of supplements, but they offered only temporary relief from her pain. When her business partner brought Dr. Blevens to their holistic nurse-sponsored conference, she jumped at the chance to hear him and brought both of her daughters along. Teresa already had an understanding of the mind/body connection to illness, but she hadn't understood the Principles behind it till she had an insight during Dr. Blevens's presentation.

> "What stood out at that conference was that we grossly misunderstand the true nature of resilience. I realized that thought, as a Principle, is the constant cause of our moment-to-moment experience of life. More succinctly,

'My thoughts create my life.' It is neither our job, nor is it in our power to fix other people, even if we love them. It was a huge turning point for me to realize that I can love them unconditionally without trying to fix them. This insight allowed me to see the mind-body connection between my stressful thinking and my chronic pain. I had a physical feeling of releasing tension and surrendering to the truth of the Principles. I began to feel light as a feather, and my chronic pain of over five years disappeared in an instant.

"Coming from a family of worriers, I began to realize that worry was not love, as I had long believed. I started to see that the door of life opens inward, not outward. When I changed from the inside, I was able to let go of the worry that was fueling my stress. From that moment on, I became aware how my thinking in the moment was the cause of my stress, not the circumstances of my life, not my nursing work, not my family, not all those other details of life."

With freedom from stress and pain, Teresa realized that a new direction was being made known to her. Her new vocation was to help other nurses realize the powerful insights that had awakened within herself. She and another RN named Lynn McCright became board certified in nurse coaching and started their own nurse coaching program.

"Our job is uncovering the Principles for our clients," Teresa told me, "helping them to see that our human experience is created from the inside out through the unchanging Principles of Mind, Thought, and Consciousness. This is the cure for the burnout and stress which have been negatively affecting members of our profession. Gaining these insights leads to transformation and healing."

I asked her how she sees the healing power of the nurse:

> "The essence of nursing, the reason we all took up nursing in the first place, is *caring for people*. We have become so distracted by all the details of nursing—coordinating with the doctors, ordering meds, electronic record keeping, documenting legal considerations, and keeping up with technological developments—that we have all become sidetracked and lost the essence of nursing. We have forgotten that nursing is *caring for the patient, mind, body, and spirit.*
>
> "The Principles help me and my colleagues to get back to our essence, our calm center. Instead of working from a stressed state of frenzy, we are able to listen and effectively respond to the patient's needs from a flowing, calm state, one step at a time. New energy, new presence, new life, new inspiration comes as a result of understanding the Principles. I experience a deeper connection to my patients and am able to be in a state of loving presence even if they are dying because I know that they are completely resilient within."

Teresa gave a lovely example of this. She had to care for an unstable patient who was in serious condition after coming out of surgery. During those critical six hours, Teresa held the patient's hand as she completed all the tasks necessary to care for her, all the while reassuring her that they would get through this together. When the patient became stable, the patient told her, "I wouldn't be here without you, because of your loving presence and reassurance."

Teresa continued. "Our love and energy can be felt even when the patient is unconscious. Caring is connecting at a deep level to carry hope to them and for them even up to the moment of death. When they are afraid of dying, I can redirect them from fear to hope and help them to let go and die in peace."

I asked Teresa how she coaches other nurses to reawaken their resilience:

"I help nurses listen to, hear, and then trust their innate wisdom and insights by teaching how the mind works through the Principles. Step one is self-care. You have to experience the Principles insightfully yourself before you can pass it on. Step two is to get past your overthinking or intellectualizing the Principles to see the deeper order of resilience. Listen to the patient, they have the answers they need, we hold space for them to see it for themselves. As one nurse in our class said, 'I am my own pressure cooker! Circumstances don't cause my pressure; my thinking is the cause.' "

I asked Teresa one last question, "How can the Principles help the healthcare system keep its bearings and prevent stress and burnout in order to have a caring presence?" "I would tell healthcare workers to not be afraid of their own experience," she responded.

"When my hospital was preparing for our first Covid-19 patients, I became caught up in my thinking about all the unknowns: fear of what this virus might mean for me personally and the ones I love; and fear of losing one of my family members or friends, or even the possibility of dying myself. All of these seemed to be real options.

Back then, there was constant change; my schedule changed five times in one day. Our resources, personnel, and PPE protocols shifted with the wind. Confusion and overload were the order of the day, and this was even before we had our first patient! At the same time, the New York nightmare was peaking and everyone was freaking out. PPE was in short supply, one mask had to last us a whole week, and we feared that we might die helping others.

"I got caught up in my thinking of all the what-ifs. I knew I was caught up in my thinking, but I couldn't seem to stop it. I forgot that I was the thinker and my thoughts were playing a role in my upset state of mind. This terrifying situation looked like an exception to the rule. I couldn't get my bearings; I had gone down the rabbit hole of believing my thinking about made-up scenarios of what might or could happen. I knew I was suffering, and I wanted relief.

"I called my coaching partner Lynn, completely upset. 'Teresa,' she said, 'you are as safe in this moment as you've ever been.' And I knew she was right. It was like the sticky fog of outside-in thinking lifted off me. I could see again. I knew that I had just become caught up in my thinking again. My fears still seemed real, but now I could see the truth of where they came from, my thought in the moment.

"When I got it all in perspective again, I realized that we as a profession had weathered so many other health crises through so many generations. We had survived the 1917 flu, polio, measles, and many other epidemics. This pandemic is no different than in times past, but this time, I am here to experience it in the present moment. This simple yet profound realization brought me back to my resilience. I know that I can handle whatever shows up in the future, I know my wisdom will show me how to deal with it in that moment."

Teresa paused. "Living in the unknown—it's a great place to be!"

(Teresa's next dream is to create an app on resilience for healthcare workers. She hopes to include many real-life stories to encourage other caregivers. Stay tuned for news of her projects at her website www.nursecoaching.com.)

Ordinary Awakenings: As I listened to these healthcare professionals, I was brought back to the deep, quiet "eye of the hurricane" within me. I believe we all can take a fresh look at our lives after hearing their experiences. We may be facing financial uncertainty and disruptions in our jobs or businesses, whether as owners or employees. We may be struggling with challenges in parenting or in our intimate relationships. What can we learn from the stories of these remarkable people? Let's gently reflect on our wisdom and its guidance in the midst of dark times, even when we don't see it and our resilience feels so far away.

CHAPTER 10

FINDING THE "EYE" OF INSIGHT AND WISDOM IN BUSINESS AND ORGANIZATIONS: WORKING SMARTER, NOT HARDER

In my second book, *Slowing Down to the Speed of Life* with Dr. Richard Carlson, we included a chapter entitled, "Working Smarter, Not Harder," that applied the Principles to the world of work. Such a large fraction of our lives is spent at work, making a living, fulfilling our ambitions and purpose. For many of us, work has become stressful, exhausting, and often overwhelming. I was raised on the belief that the more stressed I was, the more likely I was to succeed. I now see that working from a calm and inspired mind is one of the main secrets to success. The old saying "Happy go lucky" is so true. When we are in our resilient mind, we see the bigger picture, we have more creative and innovative ideas, and we see unlimited possibilities instead of obstacles getting in our way. The following story is about an organization whose purpose is to help business leaders understand the nature of their minds so that they can respond to the ever-changing landscape of the business world with a quiet mind and insight.

Insight Principles, Inc., is a consulting firm in Boston and London that has the objective of bringing success and wisdom to the corporate world. The dog-eat-dog competitive world of business seems a strange place in which to find the understanding of the Principles having such a huge impact. However, it makes sense that human performance, whether in business, sports, or daily life, is directly tied to the power of the human mind. Correctly using our minds as they were designed to function can have a huge impact on all areas of our lives. Out of curiosity, I decided to interview the Insight Principles team to learn from them how insight is the key to success and performance.

Sandy Krot, a consultant at Insight Principles shared with me how the Principles' paradigm shift is fundamental to a better approach to business:

> "I don't think we can emphasize enough how pervasive the belief is that thinking hard, pushing yourself, and imposing your will on others are the key ingredients to solving problems in the business world. Pressure and stress seem inevitable, even required. When we share the Principles, we point to an understanding that is completely foreign to many in the business world, so we have to do a lot of bridge-building and connecting of dots in order to win them over.

> "Recently, I worked with a leader who was promoted to a new role. It was a steep learning curve for him, and he had to pick up new skills quickly since the company was going through a major restructuring and the business was tanking. My client, I'll call him Bob, always considered himself the underdog. Bob's strategy for success was to push himself harder and harder. He told me, 'If I don't feel stress, something must be wrong.' Bob put in grueling hours trying his best to catch up. He didn't see his family much and was sleep-deprived. Though this strategy

had worked for him in the past, it always had taken a tremendous toll. This time was no different. When I met him, he was struggling and circling the drain.

"After Bob began to have insights into how his mind worked, he changed dramatically. He saw the thought-created nature of stress. He told me, 'I thought stress came from working hard, but it doesn't. I create my own stress through thought, and I don't have to.' That one insight, disconnecting the feelings of stress from job difficulty and recognizing that his feelings were internally generated, removed his wound-up thinking. He became clear-minded and focused in his meetings. 'Everything just flowed,' he said. Not surprisingly, before this insight, he would never ask for help. Now he was full of questions and utilized his competent team to fill in the gaps. His learning curve shot way up, his performance improved, and his stress disappeared."

Robin Charbit, CEO of Insight Principles put it this way:

"The business world is all about performance and success. In business, the bar is always being raised; what was good enough yesterday is not good enough today. 'Harder, faster, more' leads to a high level of stress, which we usually consider 'a necessary part of business.' When we come into a company and point clients to the true spiritual nature of life, they learn two things:

- They don't have to be reactive to life circumstances, allowing their stress to diminish.

- When they are more balanced, the deep wisdom of life becomes visible and flows through them. They have all the skills necessary to be successful. Our clients also find that this understanding has collateral benefits in their personal life with family, friends, and children.

"We've found a way to talk to the business community in a manner that makes sense to them. Most businesspeople are not looking for a deeper understanding of their minds and haven't even considered this as relevant. So we first show them how this understanding can enhance their performance, something they had not realized before. They come to see how this understanding can raise their game in the increasingly unpredictable, chaotic, and stressful world of global business."

My discussions with Sandy and Robin impressed me. The demand for their services keeps going up, largely because an understanding of the Principles is the "secret sauce" that allows businesses to remain competitive, reinvent themselves, and stay nimble in the hurricane of the ever-changing world of business. Gaining an understanding of how the mind works also helps those caught up in the thick of business to retain their human values, such as kindness, fairness, and respect for others. Humanity often leaves the room when the stressors of business cause people to behave selfishly, aggressively, and cruelly. Restoring this humanity in business relationships only works in companies where leaders champion these core values.

I asked Ken Manning, president of Insight Principles, how they help companies, CEOs, and stakeholders see the relevance of the

Principles in the real world of business. "We want to help them use their minds in the most effective and efficient way possible," he said.

> "There is a great amount of inefficiency with a stressed mind, which compromises communication, teamwork, decision-making, and problem-solving. We have found a way to explain to businesspeople the science of how the mind works, how to use it well so that they gain more common sense, insight, and clarity. Leaders become committed to using their minds in a healthy way before solving problems and making big decisions. We don't give advice on what to do, which is how most business consultants make their living. We teach them how to use their minds optimally so they can insightfully and strategically solve pressing issues moment to moment."

I appreciated the way one of Sandy Krot's clients expressed new insights:

> "What I learned from you about my mind is now becoming second nature. I don't have to think about it. It's just natural; it's how I operate now. Gaining an understanding of the Principles removes the barriers that block our natural resilience. The consultant's role is to educate and point out that when their clients are in their healthy mind state, they will be able to experience what is within them. This gives them the ability to solve intractable problems in a way that is more effortless and more successful with less wear and tear."

"We start every conversation with, 'What are you trying to accomplish here?' " Robin Charbit explained.

"Then we build a bridge toward their business goals, such as specific quotas, percentage increase in sales, and so forth. We have to make the discussion relevant to them before they can see how an understanding of their minds can help them.

"Here's an example of a client of ours, a European business leader struggling after the Covid-19 pandemic hit. This company, which is headquartered in Milan, Italy, conducted 80 percent of their business with the airlines. Milan was one of the places that the pandemic first hit the hardest, and their business took a big hit.

"At first, they tried to weather the storm, but soon they realized they would have to completely reinvent their business rather than just hunker down until the pandemic was over. Fortunately, thirty of the company's top executives had just completed training in our Insight Synergy Program a month earlier. The CEO realized that they could not hang on and would have to totally restructure their business model. It was like if a person had kept selling Betamax tapes after the CD was invented—game over, time to shift direction, and fast.

"The company began the process of reducing their workforce by 20 to 30 percent, closing facilities and changing their operational model (how they make money). This company reorganization would normally take months to years. Because of their understanding of the Principles, they were able to power through this all in only six weeks.

"By focusing on the mind and on the feeling [state] they were in when they made crucial decisions, the team was able to more effortlessly see common sense solutions to the immense problems they faced. They would start each day with the leadership team and check in with each person. The team would not move forward until each person was in a quiet, non-stressed mindset. After settling into the right mental space, the team would quickly come up with effective solutions.

"One insight that came to them was instead of firing 20 to 30 percent of the workforce, they asked for volunteers to retire early with a generous package. This allowed them to achieve two-thirds of the downsizing needed, but with honor, dignity, and respect, thereby preserving the morale of the workforce. During that period, they discovered new ways of reinventing themselves. This creativity resulted in several billion dollars' worth of new business contracts which replaced the lost revenue from the airline industry. They also invented two new products to launch in 2021 to replace the lost business. Keeping their eye on the ball, that is, working from their mindset of calm resolve and clarity, made this all possible."

While undergoing this transition, the Insight Principles team met with them every two weeks to keep them on track. The executives decided never to make a decision until they had a wiser perspective. Whenever they felt stuck, we would point them toward the wisdom already within them to solve the problem at hand. If someone lost their bearings, either the Insight Principles consultant or someone from the leadership team would point them in the right direction, and that would reset their thinking.

Initially, their parent company refused to go along with their plan to downsize through "self-retirement." Rather than becoming hurt or upset, the managers politely acknowledged the parent company's concerns, took some time to reflect, and returned to the table some time later with a logical plan addressing the parent company's issues. Even though the revised plan kept the essential elements of the originally proposed plan intact, this time, the parent company agreed.

The company's managers implemented their wisdom-based strategy, and in so doing, ended up saving a lot of money in the process of reinventing the company, while provoking very little ill feeling among the employees. It was a win-win for all—not only did employee morale secure the company's future, the employees' positive state of mind rippled out to their families and communities.

"An understanding of the Principles was so helpful to the leadership team and employees that they decided to offer webcasts to all their employees and their families. The Insight Principles team did ninety-minute webcasts on what had helped them manage this crisis, while also teaching the Principles. One employee shared that while he and his wife were listening to the webcast at the dining room table, their granddaughter was sitting quietly nearby coloring. Later that evening the seven-year-old girl said, 'We should all share how we are feeling (with the pandemic and lockdown). I am very frightened.' Her grandfather was amazed at how she had been impacted even though she hadn't seemed to be listening. He was struck by how the Principles are so simple that even children can be impacted. The Principles continue to cascade throughout the company and have a momentum of their own. Wisdom lies within the heart of every human being."

—Robin Charbit, CEO

Ordinary Awakenings: Can you see the impact of how you and others show up as parents and how that can impact our children and grandchildren even though we aren't consciously teaching them?

CHAPTER 11

TRANSFORMING OUR CHILDREN, PARENTS, TEACHERS AND EDUCATION

"Education is the most powerful weapon which you can use to change the world."

—Nelson Mandela

Children are our future. Whether we are parents, teachers, police, clergy, or volunteers, we all want to invest all our love, wisdom, and guidance into preparing children for life. Children are like seeds that have all the potential of mature plants, and they realize their full potential through practicing principles of gardening or horticulture.

Raising children with an understanding of the Principles of resilience allows those seeds to grow and helps them realize their purpose, talents, happiness, and success in life. Without an understanding of the Principles behind resilience, we are handicapped in nurturing that resilience as influencers in their lives. This chapter will share stories of how the Three Principles are transforming parenting, education, and counseling of children.

I am thrilled to have interviewed so many extraordinary parents, educators, and school counselors whose jobs as influencers have been immensely facilitated by gaining an understanding of inner processes, first for themselves, and then passing it on to the children. This is how we will change the world, as Nelson Mandela suggests. I will begin with the powerful story of a mother of a child with autism that dramatically demonstrates the potential of this understanding for parents with an extreme example. Here is Mary's story.

A PARENT OF A CHILD WITH AUTISM MOVES FROM LIVING IN HELL ON EARTH TO FINDING HEAVEN ON EARTH

Prior to gaining an understanding of the Principles, Mary's life was a struggle every day. When she discovered the Three Principles, her life was transformed. Mary's understanding of the true source of her feelings freed her from the prison of her own thinking and gave her an equanimity that was only fleeting prior to this realization. Mary shares her transformation:

> "Life before the Principles had moments of joy, but my existence mostly felt horrible. My son Adam, who is now twenty, was born with autism. For the most part, it was a battle because I had to live for two people, taking care of myself plus tending to his feeding, along with his outbursts, and frequent waking up at night. My life was overwhelming, and there was literally no time for me. I felt conflicted, trapped in this difficult reality, while really loving my son at the same time.

"When you live in an 'autism household,' the simplest things can be a massive task. Adam could become very distressed if things weren't done a certain way. Food had to be served just so, dressing him was a set ritual, and so forth. These were the blackest of times. Death sometimes seemed like a better option to me rather than having to face yet another day.

"Regular families didn't have to go through this. Most parents don't have adult kids who throw food against the walls. They don't suffer through sleepless nights, fearing their kid will wake up and start screaming. It was like having a newborn, but with the exhaustion lasting for years on end with no break. I felt victimized, waiting for the next trauma, the next stressful incident.

"Then I was introduced to the Three Principles through a retreat offered to parents of autistic children. Even though I had already made many positive changes in my life, I still felt burdened. As the Three Principles started to become insights, my misery literally disappeared. My constant thinking that Adam's autism was to blame for my unhappiness suddenly changed. Though nothing was different with Adam and his autism, everything had somehow changed. I had been to many other autistic retreats and temporarily felt better, but after the Three Principles retreat, the relief didn't go away. It's been two years, and I have to say I am living in a state of grace. Nothing has changed in my circumstances, but something shifted in me during that retreat.

"When I was younger, I was afraid of becoming one of those spiritual people who are detached and lack emotions. My mother would say, 'People who are heavenly goodness are of no earthly use.' I didn't want to be one of those holy types because I love my feelings. Laughter has gotten me through so much in life. But after this retreat experience, I didn't lose my humanity, nor my laughter and other emotions. What I've got now is heaven in my home. It wasn't up to me to achieve this feeling, it just came naturally on its own. There was nothing to do. The thoughts of fear and worry that were holding me down just simply fell away, and what was left was this deep sense of peace and grace. I now feel comfortable in my own skin. Even when Adam is having a meltdown, the peace doesn't go away. Now I don't have to hang on clinging by my fingernails. It just is all right, whatever is happening, whether or not there is some new crisis or another angry outburst.

"I now see that the Three Principles are constants that are creating all of our experiences. Our experience of how we see the world is made up from these three constants. We are held in place by a force that runs the whole universe. That's in me too. There is an intelligence guiding all of us that is directing us to act, and we get to see life from Thought, Mind, and Consciousness. That's the only way we can experience anything. We can't experience anything without Thought. It's not something I have to do—it just is. I don't have control over my thoughts and don't have to manage my thinking. Just knowing I am creating my experience allows my thoughts to pass and allows me to not get caught up in my negative thinking. There is no judgment of my thinking and no effort. This can change the world and probably will."

While Mary still has days when she falls into the old feelings of frustration, anger, victimization, and depression, in the light of Consciousness, she is now aware of her feelings, and these uncomfortable thoughts lift with the persistent insight of seeing the actual source of her experience. When her thoughts clear, her resilience is revealed, and she now thrives in the same exact circumstances in which she used to suffer.

Today, Mary helps other parents of children with autism to move beyond coping with their perceived hopeless circumstances to gaining understanding and peace within the "eye of the hurricane."

SUPPORTING SCHOOL COMMUNITIES

When I hear stories from parents and school community personnel about how they have learned the Principles, I am filled with hope. These adults pass their knowledge to K–12 students and impact future generations.

Can you imagine if you had learned about the role of thought from your parents and teachers while you moved from childhood into adolescence and early adulthood? Think of all the security, emotional health, mental well-being, positive behaviors, and satisfying relationships you could have experienced. Various pathways created to share this understanding in school communities will be explored in this chapter. Results of research gathered from forty plus years of work in school communities confirms the positive effects on educators, students, families, and community professionals. I'm sure we can imagine how different children's lives could be with the added benefit of educational experiences steeped in the Three Principles. It would be life changing to say the least, a truly wonderful opportunity for our youth and the world.

TRANSFORMING EDUCATION: THE ESSENTIAL CURRICULUM

Barb Aust was a preschool and elementary school teacher, principal, administrator, and college professor in British Columbia for over more than four decades. When Barb met Sydney Banks in the mid-70s, her personal and professional life was forever changed by the power of his teachings.

Barb shared, "In the very early days, there was no formalized language common to this understanding—it lay in the feeling that one brought to the work. As Syd said, 'It lies within you, and if you can see that, well…it comes with a feeling. Look for a feeling. Never mind the talk, and if you can get that *aloha* feeling in you, that feeling of love, that feeling of understanding, and [if] you give that *aloha* feeling away, you give the very essence of life by giving them love and understanding.' " With Syd's words as her starting point, Barb became a pioneer in teaching with this groundbreaking way of thinking as the underpinning of her work in education.

As a school administrator heading toward retirement, Barb wanted to pass on what she had learned over the years in hopes that those new to administration would benefit from Syd's teachings as she had. Her notes to future principals became the basis for her book, *The Essential Curriculum: 21 Ideas for Developing a Positive and Optimistic Culture.*

Barb continued,

> "It begins with teachers, parents, and administrators all realizing the Principles for themselves. When we experience this personally, we see the impossible become possible. The essential curriculum is taught

by how we show up in the classroom with a feeling of love and understanding, not just with words. When we surround ourselves with that feeling, we see children and staff fresh each day. We view them as whole and resilient, not broken or defined by their labels. We don't preach the Principles. We simply live them, and that is how they are passed on.

"When we see others in a new way, it encourages them to see themselves anew and prevents them from creating self-perpetuating beliefs about themselves. Approaching children from a calm mind changes everything. We became less judgmental, more patient, and more loving with the students and our fellow staff. In a very practical way, we show them the resilience compass they already have within themselves.

"There are no throwaway people. Everyone has full human potential, and with time and patience we can encourage them to bring forth their 'Pandora's Box' of beauty, interests, passions, purpose, and opportunities. We help them let go and move into the flow of learning. We give them a voice and listen to them deeply so that everyone feels included. Trust and rapport are the cornerstones of creating a learning environment. *The Essential Curriculum* can and should be the underpinning of all education. It is the feeling that carries the positive essence of life and learning."

NATIONAL RESILIENCE RESOURCE CENTER: SHARING THE PRINCIPLES WITH SCHOOL COMMUNITIES

I visited with Kathy Marshall, founding director of the National Resilience Resource Center (NRRC) established at the University of Minnesota. Kathy explained, "At NRRC, we believe every person has the innate *capacity* for natural resilience—the ability to navigate life successfully, realized or not. The opportunity to *learn* how we operate from the inside out makes a critical difference." She also emphasized, "Research clearly indicates it takes adults in families, schools, and communities to foster student resilience. We have had great success pointing adults to natural resilience. Once they get it, they can pass it on to the children."

Adult Outcomes: I was impressed that independent focus groups show adults completing NRRC training report *enhanced mental and physical well-being, enriched inner life and reflection, improved relationships with others, and increased satisfaction with workplace or daily life.* Amazingly, statistically significant pre/post surveys of 797 adults in the NRRC program verify positive impacts including reduced stress, improved life quality, and a more secure state of mind essential to well-being and healthy living. An independent evaluator concluded tests from ten months to six years after training provide "overwhelming evidence that the changes remain intact over time. The Principles of resilience…become internalized and continue to bear fruit and effect change long after the initial training is over."

Stories of Change: Kathy has been privileged for more than thirty years to hear amazing stories from K–12 students, school staff members, parents, and community professionals. She shared several of them with me; in one, after an assistant principal's mini resilience lesson about every kid's innate capacity for resilience, a kindergartner declared, "Nobody's a burnt cookie!"

Another time, a parent wanted to know what all this "Principles stuff" was about. Her elementary-school-age child piped up during a family squabble, "You both need to learn the Principles I was taught in school!"

An eight-year-old learned the Principles while watching her mother use one of Kathy's training visuals to teach her five-year-old sister to step out of a tantrum. The older daughter redrew the visual aid drawing and sent a better version to Kathy!

In Cairo, Egypt, NRRC cofacilitators Gary Johnson and Kathy Marshall introduced the Three Principles to educators and students in a private K–12 school system. A young Muslim educator there instinctively *knew* the Principles and helped explain the understanding to her peers.

COLLABORATING TO COCREATE EDUCATIONAL MATERIALS

"Most importantly." Kathy pointed out, "NRRC collaborates with expert colleagues like Bonnie Benard, Barb Aust, and Christa Campsall to develop inexpensive, Principles-based educational resources that are globally accessible online." (Please see NRRC in the resources section at the end of the book.)

I wanted to know more about other programs for schools. Kathy explained that at least three independent programs have been developed to support school curricula in unique ways. She pointed me to *My Guide Inside, SPARK Mentoring Programs,* and *Innate*

Health Education & Resilience Training (known as iheart) to explore further. (Please see NRRC resources for more, including scholarly articles specifically for schools.) These programs are explored below.

CURRICULAR RESOURCES FOR SCHOOL COMMUNITIES

MY GUIDE INSIDE FOR K–12 STUDENTS

I was awed by a high school senior's message to school boards after she completed the *My Guide Inside* course: "Mental wellness needs to be part of every school district's policies because if students do not feel they are capable to learn and don't have that emotional capacity to learn, school is not going to be successful." A classmate chimed in, "Every student everywhere should learn this!"

Coauthors Christa Campsall, Kathy Marshall Emerson, and Jane Tucker intentionally followed K–12 government curriculum guidelines and required competencies for academic credit. *My Guide Inside* (or MGI) enhances the personal well-being of students while simultaneously developing student competencies in communication, thinking, and personal and social responsibility.

Students in the program demonstrate clear success. A primary student announced, "I learned my guide inside solved all my problems. And my problem was I worried too much." Another said, "I didn't know about tornado thinking, and I tornado think a lot… now I know how to get over it." One middle schooler reported: "Almost every single idea or fact I learned in class has helped me already!" Another student said, "A thought is like a seed, it grows into a feeling that opens inside you. Now you decide to let it go or keep it…you always have a choice."

"Really, I'm just a guide," a senior peer counselor clarified. "When I talk from my guide inside—my wisdom—others begin to open up and speak from their own wisdom as well." Classmates also said: "My health and mental wellness have improved a lot." "This will help me as I leave home next year and go off on my own to college."

"They're not talking about the program or material, they're talking about wisdom!" Christa Campsall of Canada's Salt Springs Island said. "As a teacher, it could not be more perfect. That's the learning you want to see; you know they own it."

My Guide Inside includes accessible and very inexpensive elementary, middle, and secondary school student books and teacher's manuals, as well as a storybook for young children. MGI is available in print, e-book, and Kindle formats, and as classes streaming online for learning from home. MGI has been disseminated in twenty American states and twenty-three countries and translated into French, German, Hebrew, Italian, Portuguese, Romanian, and Spanish. Christa Campsall manages the program and its website featuring student and professional development resources. MGI is closely aligned with Sydney Banks's original teachings and sound education and resilience research.

SPARK MENTORING PROGRAMS (SPEAKING TO THE POTENTIAL, ABILITY, AND RESILIENCE INSIDE EVERY KID)

I am thrilled that SPARK students ages six to twenty-two show significant improvements in mental well-being, ability to communicate with others, decision-making, and problem-solving. They also develop greater compassion for others in tough circumstances. Because these students understand the Principles of how their own minds work, SPARK students are more able to bounce back from difficulties.

This story of a SPARK student's transformation inspires me beyond words:

> "What have I gotten from the SPARK program? Honestly, mentally including myself in the program didn't begin until the second or third class...I thought I was—I'm so mentally and emotionally broken—I didn't think listening to someone from the outside (positive) world could manage to affect me. The exact moment I really chose to listen and retreat from the battle of positive and negative emotions, I then realized...For me, my mind has changed in miraculous ways and to be completely open, my therapist couldn't even help my thought process change the way I take things in. My thoughts and forever way of thinking has evolved into things like, 'Don't think you're wrong 'cause his/her opinion is different.' 'We are all different people.' 'Don't catastrophize situations for no reason...evaluate and concentrate.' No one is the exact same person, which indicates that our minds are unique, our minds are what makes us who we are and the way we are. So now I know it's not what makes us wrong or right that makes us different, it's the fact that none of us share the same brain or the same exact opinion...agree or disagree. ☺ So, what I've gotten out of the SPARK program is to stop overthinking, stop telling yourself 'You're not this, you're not that.' Your mind is a maze that only one person can escape, and it's you. Don't get lost in someone else's opinion, don't let your emotions be

> altered in a way that you lose yourself to the point where everything you hear, you believe. You are you! I am me and we are different and the same. So never dwell on negativity and self-doubt."

—Falkenberg Road inmate, age seventeen

The SPARK nonprofit offers four separate programs aimed at young children (ages 5–8), children (8–10), middle school children (10–13) and high school teens (13–22). Each SPARK Mentoring Program includes Principles-based age appropriate social and emotional curriculum, opportunities for one-to-one student mentoring with a SPARK teen mentor or adult, participation in a community service project, parent materials and support, and a program evaluation component.

Brooke Wheeldon-Reece, president and CEO of the nonprofit, notes:

> "Our mission is to cultivate human potential and resilience through education, mentoring, and coaching in schools, jails, drug rehabilitation centers, and social service organizations. We have one hundred certified trainers in twelve countries. English, Spanish, and Hebrew translations are available. Our teen mentoring program and latest published research met the rigorous standards of the Collaborative for Academic, Social, and Emotional Learning (CASEL). The teen program was therefore designated as a Promising Program. The remaining SPARK programs are under CASEL review."

IHEART (INNATE HEALTH EDUCATION AND RESILIENCE TRAINING)

The iheart program founded in London, England, by Terry and Brian Rubenstein, helps young people uncover their innate resilience and mental well-being. I was especially drawn to stories from nine- to ten-year-old students who completed the program in a West London primary school.

These students showed improvements in relationships, emotional well-being and resilience, impulse control, classroom conduct, and reduced anger and upset. Interview responses like these from both boys and girls are good news for parents and educators everywhere:

> "Before iheart came, I had really bad anger. I could be set off by anything...it's revolutionary what it's done for me. I never thought I would see the day when my anger would just go away in a matter of seconds. It's crazy. It's gone...my anger."

> "I spoke to my mum a bit more calmly; I spoke to her [about] how iheart helped me and she calmed down."

> "I used to get bullied a lot until I realized I should not get very emotional. After iheart, I realized I could do anything. Nobody can be in charge of me except for me."

> "It's been really helpful because I was never confident and was really shy and never put up my hand. But now I do, and I've joined clubs and stuff."

> "I used to get worried that something bad might happen every day, but iheart taught me that nothing can really make me worried or sad."

"When I learnt about iheart, I started to feel really happy."

"Iheart has helped with my friends a lot."

"It's not true that people have the power to put bad feelings inside us. I can put a good feeling in myself as well."

"I reflect on the bad behavior that I do. I used to have a really bad attitude."

"If I get into trouble, I shouldn't set off and start crying. If I do cry, go to my room, take a few breaths, read a book, and not get carried away and start smashing things."

"It's helped me with school because when I do my learning, I do not give up."

An independent survey indicates that during the pandemic, iheart trained students are retaining high levels of positive emotions, managing to remain calm, and are more likely to be very good at working together with others, even those with whom they don't agree. This is compared to 83 percent of untrained young people saying the pandemic made their mental health worse.

Brian explained the nonprofit iheart works closely with entire schools, including students, staff members, and parents and guardians, to teach the clear logic of iheart Principles. Over 7,500 young people ages ten to eighteen, more than 500 educators in 227 schools, and educational organizations in fourteen countries have participated in the iheart program. Facilitators are trained and certified, and books by Terry Rubinstein and Brian Rubinstein are available. The organization hosts an annual conference, has a robust website, and advocates for national policy to support mental wellness and enhanced psychological well-being and resilience.

(Please see MGI, iheart, and SPARK in the resources section.)

TRANSFORMATION FROM FIXER TO MENTAL HEALTH EDUCATOR

Gary Johnson, MSW, spent years working with students of all ages as a hospital psychiatric assistant, Head Start program director and assistant teacher, a prison high school teacher, a county home school supervisor, but predominantly as a K–12 school social worker. In all of these positions, Gary felt his job was to observe students and make recommendations to professionals he hoped could fix these students.

In the middle of his career, Gary attended a Wisconsin Cooperative Education Service Agency seminar on resilience along with youth prevention colleague Bonnie Cook. Gary remembers, "There, I heard for the first time that I did not need to fix kids, they were already fixed! In that moment, I turned the corner from being confused and somewhat desperate to seeing that kids already had what they needed inside! I just did not know what to do about that."

In that workshop, there was a brief mention of an upcoming National Resilience Resource Center training. Gary and Bonnie followed up and attended the 1996 NRRC program. Trainers included Dr. Roger Mills, who pioneered bringing the Principles to public housing communities in Florida and California, as well as Bonnie Benard, Carol Burgoa, and Kathy Whealdon, known nationally for introducing school communities to fostering resilience in kids, a powerful combination of presenters.

Gary then contacted NRRC Director Kathy Marshall to arrange ongoing training for his rural school community.

> "For the next twenty years, NRRC conducted training programs for staff, parents, and community change agents. Kathy helped us understand that the whole community can be impacted by using a systems approach. We continued NRRC's community-based programs through the school system augmented with special guest speakers for two decades.

> "From the beginning, as I attended a variety of Three Principles trainings with the Joe Bailey team, I experienced a noticeable change. I felt so much lighter and calmer, and it showed. What a relief it was as a school social worker, and later on as a clinician, to see the *health* in my students and clients instead of looking for what was wrong or missing in them. It transformed my work from exhausting and stressful to revitalizing and rewarding.

> "For the last twenty-five years, I and others have taught the Principles behind resilience to students, teachers, and administrators in our school system, as well as to local community service agencies. As an official NRRC cofacilitator, I have also presented in other school systems.

> "The secret ingredient in the success of our own school community is that a large percentage of staff members were living from a mentally healthy state of mind. For example, we taught a single-session class on resilience to all ninth graders as part of their health class. We

noticed that 'critical incidents' (suicides, violence, and
so on) could be resolved more easily after the training.
Educators would stay calm without overreacting, thereby
helping students to also stay calm. Over time, more
than 900 people in our school and community went
through NRRC's introductory, advanced, and facilitator
training programs, as well as supplemental special
events we conducted. Positive effects rippled throughout
the community."

After Gary retired from his position as a school social worker, he
joined a small, private counseling practice, primarily working with
youth. Seeing the resilience in each of his young clients and helping
to point them back to their innate health gave him great satisfaction.
This story from his school social worker days illustrates his way of
helping others:

"I met with a young girl in middle school who was very
despondent to the point of feeling suicidal. 'Have you
ever experienced peace of mind at any time of your
life?' Gary asked. 'Only when I ride my horse and the
wind blows through my hair. I feel peace then,' the
student said. 'Would you be interested in being able to
experience that peace more of the time without having to
ride your horse?'

"I could tell I had sparked her curiosity by then and could
sense the beginning of her transformation. In follow-up
sessions, I taught her in simple terms how her mind works,
according to the Principles. She began to improve."

"I think the biggest thing the Principles taught me is to
not be afraid of the unknown. I never need to figure out

ahead of time what I will say or do in any situation. I trust in my wisdom, and this takes much of the turmoil, worry, and stress off my mind. I see that relaxing in the moment will give me the insights I need in the future.

"I have had three strokes, and during my last, I had to go to the hospital in an ambulance. As they were transporting me, I lay looking out the window at the houses and trees passing by. Suddenly it hit me, 'I am okay no matter what happens.' I felt at peace. Now, in the time of Covid-19, I don't have a lot of worries. I see this as a time of reflection and of simply 'being.' I am no longer afraid of my inevitable death."

Ordinary Awakenings: Take a moment and reflect on your childhood—the moments and longer periods of time where you felt self-doubt, insecure, angry, alone, or troubled…when it seemed like the world was against you. What if you knew then what you are now becoming aware of by reading this book? How would your life have been different? What problems and issues could you have avoided? Multiply that times everyone: with the inner powers of Mind, Thought, and Consciousness, we could all know where our experience of life actually originates.

CHAPTER 12

SEEING BEYOND OUR DIFFERENCES AND FINDING CONNECTION IN A DIVIDED WORLD

"With Wisdom, people see beyond the filters and biases of race and culture to realize the beauty in everyone. ...Wisdom applied to society would do more than anything else to halt ethnic clashes and wars the world suffers from today."

—Sydney Banks, *The Missing Link*

Our world has become polarized in a variety of ways. Politics looks more like war than a collective effort for the common good. Opinions are more important than the truth, and we're more interested in our personal belief systems than fostering relationships and resolving conflicts.

Growing up, my family was always close, and we mutually accepted each other's different viewpoints. In today's world, many families are walking on eggshells around each other; and much to my surprise, this has become true of my family as well. My parents' best friends were staunch members of the opposite political party, and they would often have lively and informative conversations at our dinner table. They disagreed without being disagreeable and enjoyed these evenings where different points of view were exchanged. Now, it seems that we have to tiptoe around our differences so we can still maintain a relationship. We tend to live within our very neat and narrow "thought cocoons" instead of welcoming new perspectives that broaden our minds or challenge our beliefs.

In addition, where we source our information has further polarized us. We live in our own echo chambers of news and media which amplify and consolidate our belief systems—belief systems that are often increasingly contradictory to those of others. Some people call this phenomenon "living on Earth One and Earth Two." Facebook, Twitter, and other social media platforms are programmed through complex algorithms to give us a biased feedback loop that reinforces our world view. We are selectively fed information that we are likely to be interested in and with which we probably agree so that we spend more time on our devices, progressively becoming more narrow-minded and less open to other viewpoints.

My understanding of the Principles has not prevented me from falling prey to these influences, which seem to be afflicting us all to some degree. However, understanding the nature of human experience and how our "separate realities" are created gives me compassion and understanding for what is happening around us. This current state of divisiveness stems from absolute innocence and a misunderstanding of the Principle of Thought and the fact of distinct personal realities.

I still struggle at times to see the innocence in others, who, from my perspective, are doing harm to themselves, others, and the world we live in. However, I more readily catch myself as I remember again where my judgment, anger, and irritation are coming from, namely, *my thinking in the moment*. This helps me to navigate the world of separate realities more effectively and bridge the gaps between our differences.

When I see where my experience and emotions are coming from, my mind quiets and settles. I am better able to listen intently and connect on a deeper level with those who might not share my beliefs. When confronted with a difficult conversation, I can hopefully become curious about their worldview and try to understand where they are coming from rather than challenge their beliefs. This often leads both of us to embrace our common humanity, even though we may believe differently. We all fundamentally want the same things, like security, love, meaning, purpose, and connection.

Remember the story in chapter 8 where the prisoner who attended Beverley and Cathy's classes on the Principles had an insight about the guards? He saw past the guards' uniforms and realized that they were just like him, operating from the same human Principles. It allowed his outlook to shift from hate to cooperation, and he gained a new respect for the guards. He saw beyond their differences to the common denominator of shared humanity.

In this chapter, I will share stories on the theme of "Seeing Beyond Our Differences" so that we can find our way out of this present era of division and start to thrive in the *eye of the hurricane* despite the winds of arguing, stalemates, and alienation between loved ones. In the end, we can and must find our common humanity and oneness.

LOVE THY NEIGHBOR: A STORY OF HEALING THE DIVIDE

I interviewed Judy Sedgeman, a friend and Three Principles colleague, about her experiences of human connection during these times of division. She shared this perfectly illustrative story, taking the topic to a new level.

> "Over time, I've become friends with my next-door neighbor. She's very likable and friendly and seems to be genuinely caring and loving. We get along well and have many things in common. For instance, we are both the same age and have both worked in the healthcare industry in a similar capacity. Although my neighbor is busy taking care of her ailing husband, she always has time to help out someone in need, whether from the neighborhood or her church. She is a delightful contrast to my previous neighbor, who was grumpy and unsociable. I felt blessed to share our two-home condo with her living under the same roof.

> "Around the time of the general election, I ran into my neighbor going into her condo; she was obviously upset. During the conversation, she expressed concern for her candidate of choice. This was the first time in all the years we'd been neighbors that politics had been brought up. To my surprise, my friend was on the opposite side of the divide. I was speechless and didn't know how to respond. I certainly didn't want to hurt our friendship, so I kept quiet.

"Isn't it funny that as soon as my neighbor started down that road, I thought, 'Oh my God, I thought I really liked her! I still like her!' I knew I didn't want to create a rift in our friendship, so I said, 'I just want you to know I really like you, but I will tell you honestly I don't agree with you politically. However, I respect your feelings, and I'm glad you told me. We'll both vote and see what happens.'

"It dawned on me that I had never had a meaningful conversation with a supporter of the opposing party. I knew that we were experiencing separate realities in a world of our personal habitual patterns of thought. She and I will never see the world the same way. In fact, even if we came to agree about politics, we still wouldn't see it exactly the same way. For the two of us to maintain a meaningful connection, we would each have to have this understanding and accept each other.

"The next time I saw my neighbor, I asked her about herself. I sincerely wanted to get to know her, to connect, to hear what was important to her. We talked about many things, including religion. She told me about her background and that for her, church had always been a big part of growing up in the South as a Baptist.

" 'I have lots of friends of different faiths,' my neighbor said, 'and we don't agree, but I see faith as something deeper than our differences. You pick your church out of conditioning, depending on how you were raised, but the whole purpose of church, no matter what the denomination, is to share the love of God and the unknown.'

> "I continued to listen respectfully. As soon as we moved
> to the formless, spiritual part of the conversation, I
> realized we were both on the same page."

Judy found that the Principles had given her the solution for coping with potential divisiveness. She saw that when thought systems are put aside and we listen deeply to each other, we can connect in spirit.

Earlier in her career, Judy had worked at the Sydney Banks Institute at West Virginia University and had had the opportunity to learn from a number of religious leaders on campus, including a Jewish rabbi, a Baptist minister, a Hindu priest, an Episcopalian minister, and a Catholic priest. She learned from them how the Principles can be the common denominator that unites people of all faiths. "If young children of different faiths and cultures were asked to draw a picture of God," she explained to me, "the drawings would all look different. But if asked to describe the 'feeling' of God. they would probably all share the same word: Love."

Judy explained that in her view,

> "The Three Principles can give us a way to connect to all
> people of all faiths, political views, and cultures without
> promoting one faith or view or culture over another.
> Underneath, we are all of one mind and connected to
> one source. Though the form is variable, the essence is
> the same. Strip away all the externals, and you will see
> all human beings are looking for the same feelings of
> unconditional love. That's where peace is found."

Judy also went on to share with me how this understanding had allowed her to leave behind the hatred, anger, and militancy of her youth. It had helped her to rise above the divisions and separations and to focus on what people have in common.

"I still get gobsmacked by people's opinions sometimes," she told me. "But more and more, I don't want to talk about our differences. After all, the essence of each of us is love."

DE-ESCALATING A POLARIZED COMMUNITY OVER A RACIALLY CHARGED ISSUE

Gary Johnson, the school social worker mentioned in the last chapter, shared a story of the power of resilience in calming down the tension in his community over changing the name of the school's team name, the "Indians." Gary shared his story:

> "As our culture becomes more sensitive to the indolent, quiet, and antiquated racism that has permeated our country, many begin to see how certain cultural choices have been insulting to certain minorities, however unintentionally.

> "After many discussions, the student body had come to a consensus with the administration that they wanted to change the mascot name from 'Indians' to 'Mustangs.' They were all in agreement and the change was moving forward when the press got wind of the story and published it in the newspaper. The townspeople erupted with anger. People became polarized around this issue, causing hurt feelings, anger, self-righteous indignation, and division. Even families were torn apart."

Gary, representing the school faculty, supported the students and administration. As he became angry at the "closed-mindedness" of the townspeople, he paused to listen to his insight and realize where his feelings were coming from. He could see that the source of his feelings was his ego, which had been triggered, and this realization helped him to settle down. It became apparent to him that the townspeople were simply acting from their thinking, which was based on a long tradition of school loyalty and a somewhat nostalgic sense of belonging that was being threatened by the name change. Through this insight, he quit taking their anger personally. He became curious about the perceptions they were having that were causing such strong emotions and began to listen more attentively. As he did so, he again realized that as the Principles state, "We all live in a separate reality of our thoughts, beliefs, and opinions." Including himself in the same boat, he began to see that both sides were operating from well-meaning innocence.

Things eventually died down, and the issue was dropped. Fifteen years later, the school board made the decision to change the name to "Mustangs," and it was no longer an issue.

Gary began to run consensus building circles in the school and the community. He would gather a group of opposing parties around a specific issue and give a brief talk about the nature of separate realities and how we all live in a world of thought. He would then direct the participants to sit in a circle and practice deep listening. Each person would speak, one at a time, till he or she had finished responding to three questions:

- How do you personally see what's happening with this issue?

- What's the worst possible outcome?

- What's the best possible outcome?

Once they had all had a chance to speak, the group would brainstorm strategies for how to realize the "best possible outcome" on a consensus basis. This exercise worked amazingly well even for the most polarizing issues. Gary held a feeling of calmness, which spilled over to the people attending the groups, setting a productive tone that kept them on track to succeed. As Gary discovered how to stay in his calm mind, he was able to appreciate other's perspectives on a variety of issues. He also became more adept at modeling good listening, respect, and empathy.

FINDING RESOLUTION THROUGH DEEP LISTENING IN CONTRACT NEGOTIATIONS

In the late 1990s, I was hired by North Memorial Hospital in Minneapolis to help change the hospital's culture of stress and burnout to one of caring, as it once had been. During that time, negotiations had broken down between the nursing union and administration. All Twin Cities hospital nurses were on strike.

As consultants to the hospital, Mavis Karn and I were asked to prepare the nurse negotiating team for these crucial meetings. We spent several sessions teaching them how to listen deeply to the opposing party. The team then took these skills with them to the negotiating table.

Knowing that the upcoming negotiations could become contentious, the team was nervous, imagining all the worst-case scenarios. As the sessions took place, representatives from each side calmly listened with open minds and respect. The nurses felt that their concerns and demands had been heard. They achieved what they felt was a fair settlement, and both sides left feeling they had "won."

While the other nursing union negotiating teams were deadlocked for weeks, ours was the first hospital to settle on a contract. The other teams were upset that we had settled so soon. By operating from the "eye of the hurricane," our nurses had been able to approach the meeting from a non-adversarial stance, which inspired more openness from the opposing side.

One nurse said, "I could see into why they thought the way they did even if I didn't agree. Their position didn't seem fair to me, but I didn't call them out. I felt empathic and nonjudgmental, and none of our earlier fears materialized." She was astonished how easily the negotiating process had gone. No one was the "enemy."

When we see where our emotions are coming from—inside our mind from the power of thought—we are able to see beyond our differences and move to a win-win solution.

PRISON AND GANG KIDS FIND COMMON GROUND—AND DISCOVER WHO THEY TRULY ARE

"...The kids learned in class that they aren't what has happened to them. They aren't their bad habits. They aren't their diagnosis. They are pure potential, there's nothing wrong with them."

—Mavis Karn, LSW, MA

Mavis has worked extensively with troubled kids in prison in the Minneapolis area. For a few years, she worked with an organization called The Missing Link, which had a contract with Red Wing Reformatory, a prison for youth under eighteen. She taught classes with a group of residents on a weekly basis for a period of two years. After these young offenders were released from prison, they attended a recidivism prevention group with Mavis. The impact of her group meetings far exceeded her expectations.

"On one occasion, I had about sixteen kids from a variety of local gangs and prisons in the area. At the beginning of the class, one of the kids sitting next to me asked me, 'G, can I talk?' (The kids called me 'G,' short for 'OG,' which means 'Original Gangster.')"

"Sure."

He pointed to each one of the others, saying their name and sometimes their gang affiliation. "It used to be that y'all were my enemies, but now in my heart I have love for all of you."

I thought they would snicker, but they didn't say a thing for a minute or two. One by one, they began to talk about what the world would be like if everyone could learn what they now knew. They imagined a world without war, because people wouldn't hate anymore. There wouldn't be fighting, racism, or poverty. There might be gangs, but they would be gangs for good.

I never said another word for the rest of the hour, and neither did my two interns. After the class was over, the kids all went out for a pizza together. My interns and I sat in awe taking in what had just happened.

After Mavis related this incredible example of how discovering who you are and how we are all different yet the same can change all of our relationships, she then told me about a time when someone asked her, "How do you work with kids from the streets, prisons, and gangs when you don't have anything in common or speak their language?" The answer was quick and easy for Mavis: "If I had to think exactly the same as someone else in order to connect with them, I'd have no one to talk to!"

I was taken aback by her response, recognizing that it's a perfectly succinct example of the separate realities that Syd Banks talked about in explaining the Three Principles. We reminisced about Syd's visits to Minnesota, and in particular, one visit when we'd joined Syd for lunch. He loved hearing stories about the many changes the Principles made in people's lives, especially those less fortunate. Hearing that Mavis had worked with kids in prisons and gangs, he turned to her with a smile and said, "Tell me some stories."

After Mavis recounted several of the kids' stories, Syd was visibly moved. He leaned across and put his hand on Mavis's arm.

"Don't ever forget the miracles, dearie."

Ordinary Awakenings: We all come from the same Source of life, and in realizing this oneness we feel connected. Can you imagine if we could all learn to truly listen to each other with curiosity instead of judgment, and how this would allow us to see beyond our differences? Imagine how this could affect our significant relationships, our work life, and our communities, as well as politics and major events on the world stage. Imagine how that could lower the temperature in our divisive arguments and help us come to consensus agreements, or at the very least, respectfully agree to disagree. Consider what this might look like in your life.

ACKNOWLEDGMENTS

When I think of who has helped me to write this book, I have to remember all the people who have encouraged me on my journey to realize my calling to help others as a psychologist, teacher, and writer. The list is long and not limited to those whom I will mention here. So many people influence us in life through their example, their belief in us, and encouraging us to trust in ourselves and our own inner wisdom.

My journey as a psychologist began with my Aunt Milly, a Catholic nun who inspired me with her courage, love, and passion for helping alleviate the suffering of humanity. She awakened that calling in me by her example; instead of becoming a priest when I briefly considered studying at a seminary, I began studies in psychology and eventually became a clinical psychologist and therapist. Early on in my career, Jacqueline Small, an extraordinary teacher and writer, saw my potential as a trainer and hired me in my first job as a trainer of counselors. I later studied with Dr. Carl Whitaker, the renowned family therapist, as well as with Virginia Satir, a gifted speaker, therapist, and writer; they became my mentors. I had a successful private practice and an active public speaking career in my early thirties; then I met Sydney Banks.

Meeting Syd was a paradigm shift, as my supervisor Dr. Whitaker called it. Everything I had come to believe in was turned upside down. I began to become more of a mental health educator than a therapist working with mental health and other issues. I realized my own mental health and freedom from stress and was able to direct others to their own innate resilience.

My career exploded, and I helped start a mental health center where I trained hundreds of therapists in this new paradigm in psychology. Eventually, at age forty, I began to write at the encouragement of Tom Grady and published my first book, *The Serenity Principle*, with HarperCollins in 1990. This began my career of writing books to help people suffering with mental health and addiction issues. After five books, I thought perhaps my writing career was complete.

Last year, Mango Publishing bought the rights to *Fearproof Your Life*, my last book. During an author's forum, I spoke on my latest ideas about how Three Principles Psychology could help in our current challenging times. Brenda Knight, my editor at Mango, wrote me the next day and asked me to publish my next book with them. She and her team came up with the title: *Thriving in the Eye of the Hurricane*. I loved it, and this book was birthed as a result. Thank you to Brenda Knight for seeing my potential.

For the past nine months, many have helped me in my writing process. Mark Chimsky, my longtime editor both at Harper and on a freelance basis, helped me design the overall concept of the book, though he was unavailable to edit it due to his full schedule. He has been one of my greatest teachers in finding my voice as a writer. While in the midst of writing, I got a call from Tamar DeJong, an editor who'd heard I was writing this book. As a student of the Three Principles who had edited other Three Principles books, she volunteered to edit this book. What a blessing both she and her husband Bruce have been in "polishing my gem," as my very first editor described the editing process. I can't thank my greatest "truth" editor, friend, and true love—my wife, Michael—enough. She has been there for me in the moments of being stuck and discouraged, always believing in me when I doubted myself.

I am grateful to Michael Neill, who crafted a beautiful foreword to *Thriving in the Eye of the Hurricane*. He is a gifted writer, coach, and speaker on the Three Principles and has helped people all over the world with his books and programs. I also want to thank my marketing team, Ann Hofferberth and James Braun, for their dedication to my website, video production, and social media, which will be a huge help in getting this book out into the world.

Lastly, I want to thank all the amazing people who were willing to share their stories of transformation here. You all inspired me to write this book in order to demonstrate the power of Three Principles Psychology to awaken the innate resilience in all human beings. I want to thank Mahima Shrestha, Dr. Amy Johnson, Dr. Richard Carlson, Jacqueline Hollows and the Beyond Recovery Boys, the staff of Mayo Clinic Arizona who participated in the Arizona Resiliency Program, along with Dr. Wyatt Decker who invited me to do the program, Peter Mears, Grace Kelly, Chana Studley, John El-Mokadem, Debbie Milam, Bryan Johnson, Beverley Wilson Hayes, Jerry Williams, Louise O'Dalaigh, Teresa Walding, Sandra Krot, Robin Charbit, Ken Manning, Barb Aust, Kathy Marshall, Christa Campsall, Brooke Wheeldon-Reese, Terri and Bryan Rubenstein, Gary Johnson, Mavis Karn, and the staff of Gulf Breeze Recovery Center. Lastly, I want to thank many others who contributed but remain anonymous.

In deepest gratitude to all of you,
Joe Bailey

AUTHOR BIOGRAPHY

 **Joseph Bailey**, MA, LP, is a licensed psychologist, seminar leader, consultant to organizations, executive coach, and licensed psychologist. He is also the bestselling author of five books, and he has taught the Three Principles Psychology throughout the world for the past forty years. Joseph received his BA in psychology cum laude from St. John's University and his MA in psychology from Texas Tech University.

Joseph developed a pilot program in resiliency for healthcare professionals at the Mayo Clinic Arizona from 2014 to 2018. Joseph's work in the healthcare field has included cultural change consultation to hospitals and healthcare systems in Michigan (East Lansing) and Minnesota (North Memorial Hospital, Golden Valley), where he taught the principles of resiliency to healthcare providers at all levels. In 2002, he helped start the Inner Life of Healers Program at the Center for Spirituality and Healing at the University of Minnesota School of Medicine. In this pioneering program, he led seminars and retreats for doctors, nurses, and other healthcare professionals on self-care, resilience, burnout prevention, and vocational renewal.

Joseph also consults with many other types of organizations, including addiction treatment centers, businesses, social service agencies, and educational institutions. He coaches leaders from all types of professions. He did staff training and program design for several addiction treatment centers, including Gulf Breeze Recovery, Florida, Farnum Center, New Hampshire, and Cedar Ridge Treatment Center, Minnesota, to name a few.

Joseph was the owner and executive director of the Minneapolis Institute of Mental Health, as well as its clinical director (1983–1995). He was the founder and president of the Foundation for the Advancement of Mental Health. He has helped develop and train the staffs of many addiction treatment centers. In addition, he has taught at the University of Minnesota's medical school as an adjunct professor at the Center for Spirituality and Healing, as an adjunct professor in the field of addictions at Metropolitan State University, and at St. Mary's University. Throughout his career, he has maintained a private practice, counseling individuals, couples, and families. He continues to write at his cabin in the Canadian wilderness.

Joseph has toured nationally to promote all his books, appearing on *CNBC Nightly News with Brian Williams*, *NBC Morning Show* (New York City), *Fox TV Morning Show* (Boston), the WCCO CBS special "Slowing Down to the Speed of Life," KMSP TV (St. Paul), KARE TV (Minneapolis), WCCC radio KBEM (Minneapolis), KMHL (Minneapolis), KNUS (Denver), KBYR (Anchorage), WNYU (New York City), KURV (Texas), WMAQ (Chicago), KUIK (Portland, OR), KPPT (Newport, OR), Talk America Network, public television (Los Angeles, CA), WWRC (Washington, DC), and numerous other radio talk shows.

Joseph has been quoted in *USA Today*, *Chicago Tribune*, *Minneapolis Star/Tribune*, *St. Paul Pioneer Press*, *Minneapolis/ St. Paul Magazine*, *Newsweek*, *Family Circle*, *Shape*, *Reader's*

Digest, Entrepreneur of the Year Magazine, Bay Area Parent, and *The Oregonian.*

Joseph has been an in-demand speaker in the United States as well as many other countries, including the UK, France, Switzerland, Spain, South Africa, and India. He speaks on podcasts and webinars internationally, and his books have been translated into twenty-six languages.

You can learn more about Joseph and his work at his website: joebaileyandassociates.com.

RESOURCES

GENERAL RESOURCES ON THREE PRINCIPLES PSYCHOLOGY

Joe Bailey and Associates—Author, coach, counselor, public speaking, training, blogs, and pioneer in Three Principles Psychology: www.joebaileyandassociates.com/

- Books and Materials: www.joebaileyandassociates.com/books-and-audio/
- Author Page on Amazon: www.amazon.com/Joseph-Bailey/e/B000APK474?ref=sr_ntt_srch_lnk_fkmr0_2&qid=1617376595&sr=8-2-fkmr0

Three Principles Foundation—Sydney Banks originally discovered the Three Principles through a profound insight. This is Sydney's own website with his original materials and talks: threeprinciplesfoundation.org/ and sydbanks.com/

The Three Principles Global Community (3PGC)—A nonprofit organization that is committed to bringing an understanding of the Three Principles to people throughout the world: 3pgc.org/

Three Principles Paradigm / Dr. Keith Blevens—We teach individuals and coaches about a natural paradigm of human functioning into which anyone can have insight, one that effortlessly leads to deeper levels of mental health, resilience, and insightful thinking: threeprinciplesparadigm.com/

Heartfelt Presence—Heartfelt Presence is a completely free, 24/7 coaching Zoom room based on the principles described in this book. You are warmly welcomed to join in anytime, given space to express what you're going through without judgment, and learn this understanding of the mind which has profoundly transformed the lives of many around the world. The coaches point you back to your own wisdom and wellbeing which allows for less stress and more freedom. Everyone on the site volunteers their time so that guests can speak with a live person 24 hours a day, 7 days a week around the world. Visit heartfeltpresence.org or contact founder Linda Ryan Brach, PhD, at host.heartfeltpresence@gmail.com

Innate Evolution / Rudi and Jules Kennard—Innate Evolution shares a revolutionary 'missing link' to human potential that's creating an evolution in consciousness. Through our voluntary work, we have reached more than a million people, and have helped tens of thousands of lives get better via our programs and free media. Our dream is to help create a kinder and more humane world: innateevolution.com/

Michael Neill—Super Coach Academy: supercoachacademy.com/

RECOVERY AND ADDICTIONS RESOURCES

Gulf Breeze Recovery—an inpatient and intensive outpatient program treating people with all types of addictions. It is based on Three Principles Psychology in a holistic approach to treatment. www.gulfbreezerecovery.com/

Beyond Recovery—a nonprofit founded by Jacqueline Hollows; programs for addiction for prisons and communities, helping to reduce the stigma of incarceration and addiction: beyond-recovery.co.uk/

Dr. Amy Johnson—The Little School of Big Change: Dr. Amy Johnson is a coach and author who produces podcasts and provides training in the Three Principles: dramyjohnson.com/

Addiction: One Cause, One Solution—Recovery From the Inside Out, by Christian McNeill and Barbara Smith, MSW. To order the book: https://www.giftsofinsight.net/book

Matters of the Soul, by Bryan Johnson. smile.amazon.com/s?k=Matters+of+the+Soul%2C+Bryan+Johnson&ref=nb_sb_noss

HEALTHCARE (CH. 9)

Teresa Walding and Lynn McCright—coaching for nurses on burnout prevention. Advancing Holistic Health: nursecoaching.com

Louise O'Dalaigh—Healthcare Leader & Coach: louiseodalaigh.com

BUSINESS CONSULTING (CH. 10)

Insight Principles, Inc.—Business consulting, coaching, and training; to order the book *Invisible Power*: insightprinciples.com/

SCHOOL COMMUNITY RESOURCES (CH. 11)

These favorites are immediately searchable: *My Guide Inside (MGI)*, a comprehensive K–12 school curriculum for academic credit, by Campsall, Marshall Emerson, and Tucker, includes primary, intermediate, and secondary student books along with teacher manuals in print, Kindle, e-book, and on-demand class formats.

Educators Living in the Joy of Gratitude consists of twenty recorded webinars featuring veteran educators telling their stories of sharing the Principles with students, educators, and parents. *The Essential Curriculum* by Aust is intended for busy school administrators, while the *Introduction to the Three Principles in Schools* video series by Aust and Campsall is for educators. *Parenting with Heart* by Marshall Emerson introduces the Principles to parents in everyday language in just twenty-five pages.

Barb Aust, BEd, MEd, began quietly sharing the Principles in 1976 in her day care centers, elementary schools, and university classes. At Sydney Banks's request, Barb wrote *See Them in Their Place of Knowing* in 2004 for an educator in Scotland. Her work also includes the following publication and video:

- *The Essential Curriculum: 21 Ideas for Developing a Positive & Optimistic Culture* (2013) is available at www.amazon. com/Essential-Curriculum-TM-developing-optimistic/ dp/1489532684

- *Introduction to the Three Principles in Schools* may be seen at youtu.be/jsLp0y9f5ac

iheart (Innate Health Education And Resilience Training) / **Terry and Brian Rubenstein**—www.iheartprinciples.com/

My Guide Inside / Christa Campsall K–12 curriculum— www.myguideinside.com/mgibooks and professional development videos www.myguideinside.com/prod

SPARK (Speaking to the Potential, Ability, and Resilience inside every Kid) mentoring programs / **Brooke Wheeldon-Reece**— thesparkinitiative.com/

National Resilience Resource Center (NRRC) / director and author **Kathy Marshall**

- Three Principles resources for schools: http://nationalresilienceresource.com/Education.html

- NRRC audiovisuals, resources, and publications: http://nationalresilienceresource.com/Resources.html

- Marshall, K. (2021). Discovering resilience and well-being in school communities. In L. Nabors (Ed.) *Resilient Children: Nurturing Positivity and Well-being across Development*. Switzerland: Springer Nature.

MISCELLANEOUS CHAPTER RESOURCES

CHAPTER 4:

Michael Bailey—poetry: michaelbaileyartist.com

CHAPTER 5:

Grace Kelly—coaching online and retreats in Italy: www.gracefulcoaching.net/

CHAPTER 6:

Chana Studley—author of *Painless: A novel about Chronic Pain and the Mind-body Connection*: chanastudley.com

John El-Mokadem—coaching and chronic pain research: www.breakthroughthat.com

Debbie Milam—author of *God's Way to Stress Less: A New Way to Experience Peace, Love, and Resiliency*: www.gracelovewell.org

CHAPTER 8:

Beverley Wilson Hayes—public speaking, coaching: missbeve2@icloud.com

One Solution—programs for community revitalization and dealing with gang violence: onesolutionglobal.org/

CHAPTER 12:

Mavis Karn, MSW—Deepen your own ability to listen and share with your clients, colleagues, family, and friends. Download this free course on deep listening with Mavis: www.gracefulcoaching.net/deeplistening/

Mango Publishing, established in 2014, publishes an eclectic list of books by diverse authors—both new and established voices—on topics ranging from business, personal growth, women's empowerment, LGBTQ studies, health, and spirituality to history, popular culture, time management, decluttering, lifestyle, mental wellness, aging, and sustainable living. We were recently named 2019 *and* 2020's #1 fastest-growing independent publisher by *Publishers Weekly*. Our success is driven by our main goal, which is to publish high-quality books that will entertain readers as well as make a positive difference in their lives.

Our readers are our most important resource; we value your input, suggestions, and ideas. We'd love to hear from you—after all, we are publishing books for you!

Please stay in touch with us and follow us at:
Facebook: Mango Publishing
Twitter: @MangoPublishing
Instagram: @MangoPublishing
LinkedIn: Mango Publishing
Pinterest: Mango Publishing
Newsletter: mangopublishinggroup.com/newsletter

Join us on Mango's journey to reinvent publishing, one book at a time.

CPSIA information can be obtained
at www.ICGtesting.com
Printed in the USA
LVHW020802011021
699182LV00004B/11

9 781642 506600